HOW TO SET GOALS

with

KAIZEN
&
IKIGAI

改善

ANTHONY RAYMOND

v.: 1.0141

When we have discovered a continent, or
crossed a chain of mountains, it is only
to find another ocean or another plain
upon the further side...

Little do ye know your own blessedness; for
to travel hopefully is a better thing than
to arrive, and the true success is to
labor.

-Robert Louis Stevenson
El Dorado (1878)

This book is dedicated to my ever-energetic mother.

CONTENTS

Get the Worksheet

Anthony here. I'd just like to say thanks for checking out my book! Also, I've created a little *companion worksheet* to help put your life goals into perspective and discover your personal Ikigai (your "true calling"). We'll be using this worksheet in Chapter 3. But download it now so you'll be ready.

If you're reading this book on a Kindle or iPad, you can click the link below to get it. Or, paperback readers can type the link into your iPhone or PC.

www.AnthonyRaymond.org/312

Introduction

From time to time, you may find yourself struggling to complete a life goal. It might be a college entrance exam, a new business startup, a fitness regimen, or perhaps even a mission to find someone to marry. While personal objectives vary widely, every one of us (each nobleman, king, pauper, and pleb) has been assigned a nonnegotiable imperative:

You must set and accomplish new goals (of one form or another) each and every day, until the day you die.

To be *human* means to be a contestant in an interminable hurdle race. When you awake each morning, the race begins. After you stumble out of bed and rub your sleepy eyes, the first objective of the day will be quick to reveal itself to you.

What's on your to-do list this morning?

- Is this your first day of school?
- The day of your child's birth?
- The start of a new career?
- Will you be landing a spacecraft on Mars?
- Is this your wedding day?
- Or, perhaps today you intend to do nothing more than drink beer and watch cat videos on YouTube.

Though the size and complexity of your goals will vary throughout your life, the necessity to set new goals will persist. There will never be a day when you find yourself without a goal (of some size) to complete. Life's marathon calls upon us to jog up a perpetual incline. The race features many hurdles, grueling sprints, and occasional checkpoints at which you'll be allowed a temporary respite—a moment to catch your breath and exchange a few high-fives before proceeding down the road. As the American author David Deida wrote:

Every moment of your life is either a test or a celebration.

Hence, becoming proficient at *the art of goal-setting* is in the interest of us all.

But if this is true, then why are we all so bad at it?

- Why do we fail to accomplish our goals so often?

- Why is it so difficult to stick to a course of action, even when we know it would be in our best interest to do so?

Curiously, most of us already possess the physical and mental abilities required to accomplish impressive life goals. Think of it this way: if a mad scientist held a gun to your head and forced you to jog five miles on a treadmill each evening after work, you could probably do it. Alternatively, if you were locked in a cell with your biology textbook and told that you would be released and given one million dollars if you got an A on your next exam, then you could probably do that too.

So, why don't you?

If you're convinced that it's in your interest to implement a nightly workout regimen or study for tomorrow's test, then why can't you just *do the work* without a gun-toting psychopath looming behind you?

Usually, such failures are not the result of a lack of intelligence or stamina. Instead, we lack the conviction and willpower necessary to see a long-term goal to its completion. Unfortunately, we humans often find it difficult to engage in the self-directed pursuit of a lengthy project when there are no external drivers prodding us to action. Life goals often call upon us to pledge a daily commitment to mentally or physically strenuous activities. But, *inactivity* is the default state of man.

When our bodies are comfortable, well-fed, and safe, then our lower mind (aka our "lizard brain," "reptilian complex," or "limbic system") would prefer to remain inactive. While our conscious mind is aware of next week's looming deadline, our lower mind thinks that next week is a million years away. It lives in the *here and now*. The future is an abstract concept that doesn't require any immediate attention.

When you call upon your lower mind to spend three hours attending to something called a "biology textbook," it will invoke various emotional states (like fatigue, boredom, procrastination, or despair) in an effort to prevent you from executing such a bothersome and energy-consuming task. Your lower mind would prefer to *not* exchange its precious energy for a few tidbits of information about frog intestines—especially when the only reward for this exertion is a piece of paper with a red "A" written on it. As the adage goes:

Your brain exists to help you survive, not to thrive.

Our mind often seems to be pursuing two contrary sets of goals. The activities that we *should be doing* are often not the activities that the lower mind necessarily enjoys doing.

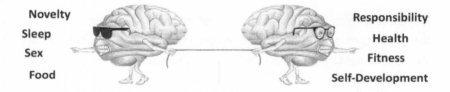

Novelty			Responsibility
Sleep			Health
Sex			Fitness
Food			Self-Development

While your conscious mind may genuinely want to engage in industrious pursuits and climb the mountain of self-actualization, your lower mind often doesn't want to come along for the ride.

- Is there any way to harmonize such divergent imperatives?
- What can we do to convince our mind to stay the course — to focus its energies on the pursuit of *constructive life goals* rather than carnal desires?

The answer to these questions lies in first recognizing the difference between *intrinsic* and *extrinsic* motivation. If someone requires you to do something (like run at gunpoint), then you are subject to an extrinsic motivator—compelled to action due to external forces of reward or punishment. On the other hand, when it comes to *intrinsic motivation*, one's actions are driven by internal desire—perhaps spurred on by the pursuit of mastery, the thrill of physical exertion, or the satisfaction of completing a beneficial objective.

- Wouldn't life be easier if there was some way to trick your mind into becoming intrinsically motivated instead of having to rely on external drivers—like a boss, a parent, or a teacher?
- What if you could learn to spot the triggers and mental traps that cause you to procrastinate, put things off, or halt your forward progress?
- What if you could change the way you perceive your life goals and learn to break objectives down into smaller constituents, such that each incremental step toward the goalpost seemed more manageable?

Well, that's what this book is here to teach you.

- It's time to put a stop to these old habits and try something new.
- It's time to stop procrastinating.
- It's time to learn how to set goals and accomplish them with gusto.

The Four Concepts

In this book, we'll be introducing you to four concepts from the east:

1. Lingchi
2. Hansei
3. Ikigai
4. Kaizen

LINGCHI

The first one, "Lingchi," is a Chinese term that is commonly translated in the West as "death by a thousand cuts." We'll be employing this metaphor throughout the book, as it so nicely describes the nature of human failure and the difficulties we encounter when attempting to identify its root cause. You may have noticed that your most challenging life problems are usually *not* the result of just one issue. Rather, they originate from a "thousand little cuts"—a thousand little ruinous decisions that come together to create a quagmire. If you learn to recognize these infractions *before* they accumulate, then you can put a stop to them—preventing undesirable circumstances from escalating into situations that are detrimental to your life goals.

HANSEI

The second concept is "Hansei" ("honest self-reflection"). Hansei is a Japanese method for understanding "what went wrong." It's about seeking clarity of thought through careful consideration of your past mistakes. When you are skilled in Hansei, then you will be better able to analyze the multidimensional failures of your past, and prevent yourself from making the same mistakes in the future.

I K I G A I

The third concept is "Ikigai." Ikigai is a Japanese life strategy that emphasizes the importance of finding your "true calling." Colloquially, the word can be translated as "your reason for living" or your "reason to get out of bed in the morning." The mindset is perpetuated by the long-lived residents of Okinawa Island—many of whom cite their Ikigai as the reason for their impressive longevity. The pursuit of one's Ikigai is an important journey of self-discovery. If you can correctly identify the vocation that you are best suited for, then the spark of intrinsic motivation will illuminate within you—igniting the fuel that powers your passions and prompting you to accomplish momentous feats.

K A I Z E N

And finally, the solution to many of our goal-setting problems can be found in the fourth concept, "Kaizen," — often translated as "continuous improvement." With Kaizen, we understand that the answers to the big problems in life do not come from a magic pill. Instead, real solutions are usually the result of years of concentrated effort and dedication. Kaizen teaches us how to atomize big obstacles; how to break them down into their more manageable component parts. And how to overcome each hurdle via continuous, gradual, and consistent daily exertion.

Ready to begin?

When you train your mind to be ever-cognizant of these four concepts, you'll have a unique perspective on goal-fulfillment—one that few people in the west have ever been exposed to. The synergy of these ideas will enable you to muster greater self-discipline, focus, stick-to-itiveness, and drive. Even your most challenging life goals may suddenly seem achievable to you.

Are you ready to get started?

Then read on, and let's take your goal-setting skills to the next level.

Ch. 1: Intro to Lingchi

The History of Lingchi

Many methods of torture were used to punish criminals and corrupt officials in Imperial China. But one particularly gruesome technique, "Lingchi," stoked the morbid curiosity of western interlopers—who would occasionally write about (and sometimes photograph) the ritual in gory detail. In English, the term "Lingchi" has been traditionally translated as: "death by a thousand cuts." In the typical depiction of the practice, an executioner uses a sharp knife to methodically cut small shards of skin from a victim's body. This happens over an extended period (for several hours or even several days), resulting in excruciating pain and eventual death. Reports of Lingchi-like procedures can be found during the Zhou Dynasty (circa 1045-256 BCE), where it was used as a punishment for egregious crimes—like treason or murder—and sometimes as a means to deter political rivals.

Western accounts of Lingchi started emerging in the 1800s:

- The English journalist Sir Henry Norman described the practice in his 1895 book "The Peoples and Politics of the Far East." However, his descriptions were based on secondary sources, as he had never personally witnessed a Lingchi ceremony.
- Four years later, during the Boxer Rebellion of 1899, French soldiers from the Eight-Nation Alliance snapped the oldest remaining photographs of Lingchi. The most famous photo was of a mentally unstable boy who had murdered his mother. Some of these images were published in 1930 by the French psychologist George Dumas in his book *Nouveau Traité de Psychologie.*
- In 1905, Lingchi was officially abolished in China but used one last time in April of the same year—to torture a Mongol guard who had murdered his region's lord. Twelve photos from this execution still exist today.

Nobody is quite sure if every Lingchi sentence was carried out in the manner described in western depictions. Some travelers have emerged from China telling horrific tales of multi-hour skin-slicing rituals, while others have insisted that the victim was already long-dead before the slicing even began. So we may never know how apocryphal our Lingchi accounts are. But, for our purposes here, we're not concerned with the ghastly historical details. Instead, we're interested in the metaphor.

The Lingchi Metaphor

In glancing at the latest newspaper headlines, it's easy to gawk in horror at the deplorable crimes that manage to make the front page. The murders, the muggings, the bank heists—these are indeed wicked acts. But they do not constitute the majority of human failings. Most of us (despite our many personal failings) are actually quite restrained. Even the most violent men among us are usually only violent for a few moments in their entire life; the rest of their time is spent in relative peace.

While it is possible that you know someone who committed a nefarious crime—like homicide, rape, or grand larceny—it's probable that you've never participated in an offense of this caliber yourself. For most of us, our lives are not defined by a single horrific act of violence. Our daily offenses never make the 5 o'clock news. Instead, our lives are burdened with a thousand little depravities, a thousand little sins, or a thousand little cuts.

As you look back at life's challenges (in health, wealth, and relationships), you'll find that personal failures are typically not the result of *just one problem*. Instead, the big problems in life, about the issues that really matter, are usually the result of many little problems—the innumerable (and seemingly minuscule) issues that we allow to accumulate year after year.

- The "little white lies" you told your spouse at the last office party.
- The extra cheeseburger you ate during the backyard barbeque.
- The weekend gym class that you were too lazy to attend.
- The wild Sunday night when you partied instead of studying for your exam.
- The Monday morning when you showed up late to the office.
- The corners you cut when you released your last product.

Taken one by one, each of these infractions is hardly noticeable. But, over time, the accumulation of these issues can result in a disastrous outcome. A thousand *little problems* come together to form a *big problem*, and your life goals are subject to Lingchi—a death by a thousand cuts.

Similar observations have been made in other cultures:

- The Roman philosopher Seneca the Younger (4 BC - AD 65) once wrote, "It is not the last drop that empties the water clock, but all that which previously has flowed out."
- In his 1684 debate with John Bramhall, Thomas Hobbes exclaimed, "[It is] the last feather [which] may be said to break a horse's back."
- Most commonly today, we use the phrase "the straw that broke the camel's back" to describe the final result of a cumulative process.

Such metaphors help to remind us of our limited ability to identify the root causes of complex problems. It's easy to blame our failures in the game of life on just one circumstance or one person—like an emotionally distant parent, an unfair teacher, an unscrupulous boss, or an abusive spouse. Truly, such toxic relationships contribute to our misfortunes. But, as you look back upon your past, can you identify the ways in which your own behaviors have been detrimental to your life goals?

- Can you envision the long chain of poor decisions—which ultimately caused you to abandon one of your pursuits?
- Can you readily identify the many lapses in judgment that you commit each day?
- Can you observe yourself making the same set of poor life choices again, and again, and again?

Indeed, becoming mindful of how and why these little violations occur is essential in developing your goal-accomplishment skillset. Your practiced ability to achieve a deeper level of self-awareness about your past transgressions is called "Hansei," which we'll be discussing in Chapter 2. But, for now, let's take a moment to list seven types of delinquencies that are deleterious to your life goals.

The Seven Deadly Sins

Through the millennia, many efforts have been made to codify the moral failings of man. One of the oldest of such taxonomies is the "seven deadly sins." Contrary to popular belief, this list does not appear in the bible. Instead, its origin is primarily attributed to the work of Evagrius Ponticus (or "Evagrius the Solitary")—a highly educated Christian ascetic who produced most of his work in Egypt from the year 385 AD till his death in 399 AD. Given that Evagrius was a classical scholar, he was able to catalog and systematize some of the existing oral teachings of the *Desert Fathers*—Christian hermits and monks who lived in the Scetes desert.

The seven deadly sins represent Evagrius' attempt to cite the seven most pernicious "afflictions," which he believed all good men ought continuously struggle to restrain. They are:

1. **Lust**: unbridled sexual desire.
2. **Gluttony**: the overindulgence (or overconsumption) of anything (food, sex, power, etc.).
3. **Greed**: the rapacious pursuit of material possessions.
4. **Sloth**: a reluctance to work or an apathetic approach to daily activities.
5. **Wrath**: uncontrolled feelings of anger, rage, and hatred.
6. **Envy**: resentment about the traits or possessions of others.
7. **Pride**: excessive hubris or misplaced self-confidence.

You don't have to be a religious or spiritual person to see the value in a life that is free of such vices. (Personally, I'm not very religious at all.) Whether or not you believe that God will strike you down after you commit any of these offenses is irrelevant to our conversation. What's paramount is that you recognize that the seven deadly sins are really just a warning against allowing one's natural faculties to be expressed to excess. When appropriately enacted, each of these behaviors has utility.

1. **Lustful** sexual desire makes human mating possible.
2. **Gluttonous** hunger prompts us to seek out sustenance.

3. **Greed** (or the pursuit of material goods) is essential in that we must own some possessions just to survive.
4. **Sloth** can prevent us from devoting energy to activities that may not result in a net benefit.
5. **Wrath** can be justified in times when self-defense is necessary.
6. **Envy** can incite us to action and drive us to improve our position in life.
7. **Pride** can be properly displayed in the form of a spirited and self-confident persona.

None of these behaviors are evil in and of themselves. It is only when they are taken to the extreme that these actions become "sins." As you think back to the times in your life when you have been susceptible to these temptations, you'll likely note that most of your misdeeds did not result in "big problems."

- You've probably never destroyed a marriage because of lust.
- You've probably never ballooned up to 400 pounds because of gluttony or sloth.
- And you've probably never been wrathful or envious enough to murder someone.

Instead, when it comes to day-to-day life, these vices usually manifest in the form of a thousand inconspicuous offenses (a thousand tiny cuts).

For example, in the life of a college student, such sins often arise in the form of productivity-destroying behaviors such as:

1. **Lust**: Watching pornography when you should be studying.
2. **Gluttony**: Spending the evening consuming a pepperoni pizza, buffalo wings, and beer.
3. **Greed**: Online shopping for things desired but not needed.
4. **Sloth**: Playing video games.
5. **Wrath**: Discursive thought about past girlfriends or current class rivals.
6. **Envy**: Harboring jealousy over a roommate's new sports car.

7. **Pride**: Proclamations that one is too smart for schooling or that homework is for stupid people.

We should take note of how inconsequential the above-listed infractions are. If you spend an evening eating pizza, drinking beer, watching porn, playing video games, shopping on eBay, and gawking at your roommate's new Mustang convertible, then it is probable that *no harm shall befall you.* (In fact, you'll probably have a pretty good night.) But remember, the Lingchi concept is defined as "death by a thousand cuts"—not just one. A single night of mildly decadent behavior never hurt anyone. Instead, tragedy usually strikes following the accumulation of thousands of such evenings, which eventually amount to a pernicious attack upon your life goals and psyche.

The Three Goal Killers

The seven deadly sins are useful for the moment-by-moment monitoring of personal behaviors. However, when it comes to identifying the actions that are most detrimental to long-term objectives, we might suggest an additional (more practical) taxonomy—the "three goal killers."

Goal Killer #1: Inactivity

Mastering the art of personal self-discipline starts with first identifying which behaviors are most harmful to our mental and physical wellbeing. It is very easy to get caught in a negative feedback loop. The farther we stray from our life path, the more we feel fatigued, anxious, and depressed. These emotions may manifest as yet more lethargic behaviors—making us even less productive. The resultant listlessness causes us to stray even farther off course—which incites yet another round of negative emotions. And so the cycle continues…

The trigger that incites this negative cascade may be physiological in nature (stemming from a lack of exercise, obesity, or drug use). Or it may be the result of a psychological ailment like depression. In either case, the inactivity that is brought upon during such episodes is detrimental to your goal-attainment efforts.

Inactivity causes us to lose valuable time.

Skipping a day of school or missing a college homework assignment might only result in mild short-term consequences. However, as we've tried to emphasize throughout this chapter, major life goals die a slow death—one brought upon by a million minor delays—the accumulation of which results in dream-killing stagnation.

One day— perhaps a decade from now—you might wake up to realize that your life situation remains unchanged or has even gotten worse. This is the most unfortunate consequence of inactivity, lethargy, procrastination, and sloth. Once your time is gone, it's gone. Mankind can create many things, but we can't create time. The amount of time available for the accomplishment of your goals is forever decreasing. With each tick of the clock, the end of your time draws nearer. This is why you must value your time as you value a diamond ring or a gold watch. It's a precious resource that can never be replenished.

Inactivity leads to hasty decisions.

When faced with an upcoming deadline, it is forever tempting to perceive the amount of time available for the project's completion as much longer than it actually is. You are most likely well familiar with this illusion. In school, you may have been asked to complete a book report by next Friday, but managed to refrain from writing a single word until Thursday at 8:00 pm. When you finally do coax your mind into working on the project, only a few hours remain available to you. So you take shortcuts—you make hasty last-minute decisions that result in inferior work. Of course, adults are susceptible to similar bouts of procrastination. But the consequences of failing to perform are all the more damaging—negatively impacting future academic, financial, and personal goals.

Inactivity causes us to miss valuable opportunities.

Often, the achievement of a grand life goal is dependent upon a serendipitous discovery—of the sort that cannot be unearthed while sitting in front of the television set. This is why consistent daily action is so essential. Because it is only by *walking the path* that *new* paths will emerge. If you remain stagnant and cease your forward movement down life's winding road, then the adventures that lie beyond the next bend will never be revealed to you.

Goal Killer #2: Toxic People

Perhaps you are fortunate enough to be surrounded by goodhearted people—dynamic, intelligent, and generous souls who genuinely wish the best for you. Many such people do indeed exist in this world. However, it is perhaps more common to meet people of the other variety:

- People who are better at criticizing than doing.
- People who try to pull you down to their level.
- People who live only for the next weekend adventure.
- People who live to drink and party.
- Or, people who have given up on life altogether.

Fraternizing with such toxic people can be detrimental to your life goals. Their intentions may not necessarily be evil; your friends and family usually do not deliberately intend to destroy your dreams or knock you from your foundation. But this world is full of lost souls—people who have dwelled in a miasma of negativity for so long that they can no longer envision what a life of abundance could possibly look like.

- Some of us are born into toxic environments—the children of parents who take little interest in their future wellbeing. Life's slings and arrows can turn a mother or father into a shadow of their former selves. Depression and addiction might incite them to violence or cause them to surrender to apathy—resigned to merely sit on the couch from sun up to sun down, watching television, eating junk food, and drinking alcohol to dull the senses.

- Alternatively, the reverse can be true. Parents can become too restrictive or too reliant upon their children's success. They might even abandon their own life goals entirely, instead electing to live vicariously through the achievements of their offspring. Consequently, such parents may be nothing more than a lurking shadow—forever critiquing their children's performance and prodding them to "be better." Unfortunately, such draconian behavior sometimes results in the opposite outcome.

- Even more commonly, you'll meet people who simply long for a life of leisure. Their goal is to do absolutely nothing. For them, a workday is just an interval of time that must be sacrificed so that they can get to the weekend. Such gadabouts are rarely capable of impressive feats. Since long-term goals (by definition) do not provide immediate positive stimuli, most people are unable to commit to them. They have trouble rationalizing the sacrifice of comforts *today* for the prospect of a momentous reward *tomorrow*. Such an ephemeral outlook will hinder one's attempt to engage in lengthy pursuits of any kind.

For these reasons, we must be discerning about the company we keep. Quests are easier to complete when we're surrounded by like-minded comrades who are willing to march in pursuit of mutually beneficial goals. As the old self-help adage states:

We are the sum of the five people closest to us.

Goal Killer #3: Crippling Fear

If you come across a bear while hiking in the woods, your body's first instinctual reaction will be to cease your forward movement. In such a circumstance, this inactivity may be the correct response, and it might even save your life. But when we allow irrational fears to continually halt our forward progress, then the emotion becomes problematic.

Fear and progress are not friends. Your lower mind wants to *feel* safe, secure, and satiated. If it senses that you are content in the present moment, then it will prefer *this* environment to any other that you would call upon it to enter.

- This is why you didn't raise your hand in class.
- This is why you avoided walking into your boss's office last week.

- This is why you didn't call that girl.

Of course, this is not to say that any of the above-listed actions would have been fruitful.

- The class might have laughed at you.
- Your boss might have fired you.
- And the girl might have rejected you, hung up the phone, and reported your failed efforts at seduction to everyone in town.

Sometimes your fears are warranted. Most of the gambits you attempt in life will fail. Some of them will fail spectacularly. And yet, a few of them will succeed fabulously and result in life-changing outcomes. Aye, there's the rub. Things might have gone swimmingly.

- Your professor might have noticed your brilliance and recommended that you attend his PhD program.
- Your boss might have liked your idea and offered you a promotion.
- And the girl on the other end of the phone might have been your future wife.

Managing risk and fear is a skill that must be honed throughout your life. As each new opportunity reveals itself, you must be ready to objectively assess its associated risk and manage your personal fears, misgivings, and doubts about the venture.

Much of the trepidation we experience in pursuit of our goals comes from the fear of exchanging our current situation for a new and uncertain one. When we feel that we are nearing a new stage of life, it is common to experience anxiety about the upcoming metamorphosis. Sometimes, people will cling to their present routine (or lifestyle, or hometown, or job)—refusing to abandon a "good enough" course of action, even if the alternate route has the potential to lead to greener pastures.

Change will forever be a part of your life. You will witness changes in governmental leadership, in national labor demands, in the global economy, and in the very nature of money itself. You will go through physiological and psychological changes. Your mind's biochemistry will change; the way you see the world now will be different than the way you see it in ten years' time. If you pick up this book in a decade, the words that leap from its pages will be perceived differently; each sentence will be winnowed by neuronal fibers that have been matured by your accumulated life experiences. Additionally, change often comes in the form of uncontrollable tragedies like sudden illnesses, natural disasters, or war. Despite our best efforts to build a protective fortress around our possessions, our barricades cannot deter every assault.

Once you come to accept the transient nature of your health, wealth, family, and finances, then the inevitable changes to these constructs need not be so surprising when they finally occur. While we must always strive to avoid undesirable outcomes, we do so with the acceptance that entropy will forever be our contender. Just as the force of gravity is an unalterable property of the cosmos that we must learn to coexist with, so too must be our relationship with change. As Marcus Aurelius wrote:

Is any man afraid of change? What can take place without change? What then is more pleasing or more suitable to the universal nature? ... Can you take a hot bath unless the wood for the fire undergoes a change? And can you be nourished unless the food undergoes a change? And can anything else that is useful be accomplished without change? Do you not see then that for yourself also to change is just the same, and equally necessary for the universal nature?

Recognize life's many vices

Have you ever known someone who showed great promise early in life, but seemed to falter later on? Perhaps this person was a high school football star, the leader of his debate team, or a talented musician. But, as the years passed by, you may have watched this person make a series of poor life choices.

- Did he drop out of school?
- Did he cheat on his wife?
- Did he get a divorce?
- Did he get fat?
- Did he spend time in the hospital?
- Was he addicted to alcohol or drugs?
- Was he ever arrested?
- Was he fired from his job?

In considering the life journeys of your friends and family, it is probable that the above-listed outcomes remind you of someone you know. Someone who succumbed to life's many temptations. Someone who allowed his health, wealth, and relationships to deteriorate—worn away by degeneracy, or laziness, or addiction, or the sands of time.

The point of this chapter has been to get you to appreciate the pernicious nature of the world's many vices. Most of our "bad decisions" are nearly imperceptibly bad in the moment. A dream is not the kind of entity that can be killed by a single well-placed blow to the head. Instead, our dreams die a slow death, instigated by a million little mishaps—most of which we bring upon ourselves. Your ability to remain cognizant of this Lingchi phenomenon—to identify the "thousand little cuts" that slice away at your life goals—is necessary for the evolution of your personal productivity skillset, and essential if you wish to avoid succumbing to the many temptations of man.

Ch. 2: Intro to Hansei

In Japanese, the term "Hansei" is comprised of the words: "Han" and "Sei."

- "Han" means "to turn over and examine."
- And "Sei" means to "look back upon in review of the past."

So Hansei could be directly translated as "past examination" or (most commonly) "self-reflection." In Japanese corporations, Hansei is sometimes employed as a team-development exercise in which participants engage in a critical analysis of their past work performance. Here, they are asked to carefully cite their own shortcomings and come up with a strategy to improve their future efforts.

You don't need to own a corporation to apply the Hansei methodology to your own goal-setting endeavors. When it comes to personal development and productivity, Hansei is similarly useful—prompting us to remain humble in victory, take responsibility for our flaws, avoid the natural tendency to cast blame on others and learn from our mistakes.

Sometimes, it is only by digging up the past that we can understand the present. With Hansei, we try to make sense of the long chain of decisions that led us to our present life situation (good or bad). In performing this ritual of practiced introspection, we hope to enhance our insight into future objectives and develop an awareness of past wrongs. As the Danish philosopher Søren Kierkegaard wrote:

Life can only be understood backwards; but it must be lived forwards.

Hansei in other cultures

The idea that one should devote time to meditative and honest self-critique is probably not new to you.

- The ancient Greeks espoused the value of reflective contemplation with the phrase **"temet nosce"** or "know thyself."
- Socrates expounded upon this concept when he offered that **"The unexamined life is not worth living."**
- The Germans have a proverb which advises **"Selbsterkenntnis ist der erste Schritt zur Besserung,"** or **"Self-awareness is the first step to improvement."**
- And, an oft-cited *Alcoholics Anonymous* doctrine reads **"The first step is admitting you have a problem."**

From time to time, we all find ourselves sitting alone and trying to understand why our past decisions led to an undesirable outcome. Hansei attempts to ritualize this process.

In one sentence, we might define Hansei as:

The practice of carefully identifying, considering, and taking responsibility for past mistakes or shortcomings, followed by the implementation of changes to ensure that these errors do not reoccur.

Our failures in life are usually the result of a long chain of poor decisions. With Hansei, we take time to carefully consider each link in this chain, and identify how our past mistakes have caused us to stray from our life goals.

Your first steps with Hansei

Step 1. Find a time and a place for quiet contemplation

We begin the Hansei ritual by devoting a block of time to a "Hansei-kai" or "reflection meeting." In the Japanese corporate world, this is a meeting of the minds in which employees engage in humble self-reflection about how a particular situation could have gone better. At Toyota, some departments insist that employees dedicate weekly hours to such sessions—especially following the completion of a key project milestone.

Of course, you are not required to sit in a boardroom during your personal Hansei-kai. Instead, your Hansei session can just occupy a few minutes of personal time—perhaps set aside before bed or after dinner. You might allocate this period on a weekly basis but you're encouraged to try doing it daily in order to make a habit out of the process.

When it comes to selecting a space for your Hansei-kai, it's best if you choose a comfortable chair in a quiet room—one in which you can sit alone with your thoughts for ten to twenty minutes.

Step 2. Review a past failure or mistake

Once you have managed to find a moment for a Hansei-kai, then it's time to engage in introspection. Start by setting a timer for ten minutes and then select a recent incident in which you failed to accomplish one of your goals. Try asking yourself the following questions:

- What was my original intent in pursuing this goal?
- What actions did I take to make this goal a reality?
- What outcome was I expecting from this effort?
- What was the actual outcome?
- Why is the expected outcome different than the actual outcome?

This initial set of inquiries should help to dredge up the actions that led to the undesirable result.

We should note that a Hansei-kai need not necessarily be devoted to a rigorous analysis of your long-term life goals. Instead, you might start by simply pondering the question, "What went wrong today?"

- Did you forget to silence your cell phone when studying, hence allowing yourself to get distracted by a text message thread?
- Did you spend too much time answering emails instead of working on your new project?
- Did your coworker insist on buying you lunch at a certain fast-food restaurant known for their 900-calorie bacon burgers?
- Did you notice the way your spouse's smile left her face when you poured that third glass of wine?

A Hansei-kai is when you should evaluate any given mishap or foible that you may be struggling with in your health, wealth, and relationships. In pondering your circumstances, it's important to focus on the way in which *your own actions* contributed to the predicament (no matter how minute).

- Can you see yourself showing up late at work or at school?
- Did you fail to check up on a coworker who is known for his forgetfulness?
- Did you rush through a report or an assignment when you should have allotted more time for its completion?

Your mind will naturally vacillate between feelings of shame and a need to rationalize your behavior. This sort of discursive thought is not productive. The goal of Hansei is not to provide you with a moment to stew in agony. If your mind begins to doddle down some ego-driven rabbit trail, then try focusing your attention on a single written sentence. For example, if there was a particularly contentious problem at the office today, then write something like the following on a piece of paper and place it in your field of view:

What could I have done to handle today's work situation better?

Allow your mind to devote ten minutes of raw cognitive processing to this single question, and try to avoid thinking about other topics until the timer rings.

Step 3. Log your negative tendencies

After performing the Hansei ritual for a few days, one of the first things you'll notice is how often you make the same set of mistakes—again and again. You'll catch yourself wondering:

- Why did I send that text message when I knew I should be working?
- Why did I neglect to verify that missing order invoice when I knew the clerk had trouble hearing me?
- Why did I walk into that pastry shop when I knew I couldn't walk out without buying something?

The manic behaviors of the mind are surprisingly easy to rationalize in the moment. This is why it's important to keep a Hansei log—a record of the specific inadequacies that you focused on during your Hansei session. By logging each episode, you will soon reveal patterns in your behaviors.

- Do you reliably commit the same infraction at a certain time each day?
- Are you more likely to succumb to temptation when a particular friend or coworker enters your workspace?
- Are your bad habits triggered by a predictably reoccurring event or situation?

Remember, the point of this process is not to punish yourself by merely cataloging your many faults. Rather, it's about learning to recognize and prepare for future circumstances in which you are prone to recidivism.

Step 4. Make a commitment to be better

There is a difference between knowing the path and walking the path. Merely recognizing your mistakes is only the first step. Correcting them is the next challenge. In this final Hansei step, you'll need to devote some thought to course correction. After you have sufficiently evaluated the nature of your mistakes, try to come up with a strategy to prevent them from reoccurring.

- Are you tempted to glance at your phone during a study session? Make a rule to leave it at home when you go to the library to study.
- Are you tempted to start a fight with your brother-in-law whenever he starts talking about politics? Make a rule to change the subject.
- Are you tempted to buy a hotdog when you pass the vendor at your building's front entrance? Make a rule to enter via the side entrance.

The longer your Hansei log grows, the more you'll understand how difficult it is to break a bad habit, and the more you'll catch yourself falling into the same trap, again and again. But, as Alexander Pope wrote, "To err is human; to forgive, divine." In Hansei, we take a rare moment to acknowledge that we are vastly flawed creatures—riddled with contradictions and burdened with whims—most of which we are only sparsely aware of. Pledging to remain cognizant of our shortcomings and to improve upon our future circumstances is the goal of a Hansei practice. As the Toyota Technical Center manager Bruce Brownlee put it:

Hansei is really much deeper than reflection. It is really being honest about your own weaknesses. If you are talking about only your strengths, you are bragging. If you are

recognizing your weaknesses with sincerity, it is [a sign of] strength. But it does not end there. [You must also commit to *change*, and strive to] overcome those weaknesses...

Five Hansei Principles

When properly executed, Hansei can function as a serene harbor in which a momentary respite is granted to your ego. It need not defend you so vehemently because you are free from social consequences during a personal Hansei-kai. In these moments, you may entertain thoughts about your own inadequacies without requiring your ego to chime in on the matter.

Of course, to be effective, Hansei requires your internal discourse to be a truthful one. You'll have to "get out of your head" and attempt to evaluate your performance with a critical eye. For many, this exercise can be challenging. However, in time we can all learn to render a more objective analysis of our behaviors and performance. Below, we've listed five Hansei principles to facilitate this process.

Principle 1. Avoid self-justification—even if you're convinced that the problem is not your fault.

Complex problems are rarely the fault of just one person. Instead, a catastrophe usually comes at the end of a long chain of errors committed by multiple people over a lengthy timespan. It is always tempting to assign the majority of the blame to another party. And, it indeed may be the case that this other party is wholly responsible. But, in Hansei, we don't play the "blame game." Instead, a Hansei-kai is a temporary safe space in which you look inside yourself in an attempt to account for the role that *you* have played in the formulation of the problem.

During this process, your mind will attempt to sweep bad experiences, failures, and mistakes under the rug. The ego scampers away from introspective analysis in the same way that mice hide when you turn on the kitchen light, and it will attempt many ploys to convince you to abandon your Hansei-kai.

- First, it will try to blame others for inciting the issue.
- Then, it will attempt to eschew responsibility for any portion of the problem that was under your control.
- And it might even try to blame everything on "bad luck" or a "bad hair day."

Such avoidance strategies are not welcomed during Hansei. Instead, we are to focus on:

1. Acknowledging mistakes and accepting responsibility for failure.
2. Finding ways to identify and halt the repetition of bad habits.
3. The implementation of changes needed to ensure that our future goals can benefit from past lessons learned.

Remember, during Hansei, we evaluate our internal world, not the external world. Even if you're utterly convinced that the problem of the day has nothing to do with you, that's still no excuse to remove yourself from criticism. Until the ten minute timer rings, you're only allowed to think about the ways in which *you* contributed to the dilemma. If you like, you can go return to blaming the other party when your Hansei session is over. But, if you actually succeed in performing Hansei for the entire ten minute session, then you may be surprised to find that you no longer hold the same degree of animosity towards the offender.

Maybe (just maybe) you could have handled things a little better.

Forcing your mind to consider alternate perspectives will help to reframe the problem—enabling you to see complex social situations in a new light. Shifting the paradigm will provide you with an alternate (and hopefully more amicable) perspective from which to gauge your performance and that of your peers. Remember, it is much easier to critique the work of another man than that of your own. Or, as Matthew 7:5 reads:

...first take the log out of your own eye, and then you will see clearly to take the speck out of your brother's eye.

Principle 2. Don't beat yourself up during Hansei

During moments of contemplation, it's easy to let our inner voice take charge—to hand over our consciousness to the discursive meanderings of our internal narrator. He's the guy who pokes us throughout the day exclaiming:

- "You can't do anything right..."
- "This assignment is too difficult for you..."
- "You're just not good enough..."

Managing the volume of this voice is a lifelong challenge. And overcoming its assault upon your psyche is not a victory that you need only win once. Instead, as we rise with the sun each day, our internal dialogue rises with us—anxious to offer criticism as we execute our daily activities.

During a Hansei session, this narrator might be eager to lead you down a path of despair and hopelessness—seizing the opportunity to berate you and flood your consciousness with doubt regarding your abilities. But Hansei is not about beating yourself up. Instead, it's about making your life better by identifying areas that need improvement. While we are all required to be honest during a Hansei-kai, we are also asked to avoid casting unproductive animus toward all parties involved—including ourselves.

Principle 3. Accept that painful memories might resurface

Our minds are laden with psychological triggers—negative emotions that attach themselves to memories like parasites to a host. As we dig up old memories during a session of Hansei, undesirable emotions (like anger, rage, frustration, jealousy, or sorrow) may be concomitantly unearthed.

As enlightened practitioners of eastern mysticism, we'd all like to believe that we are immune from the sting of such carnal compulsions. But the truth is, none of us ever really are. The evolutionary utility of human emotion is too great. This diverse pallet of passions provides your lower brain with a language by which to communicate with your conscious mind. Instead of ignoring this communiqué, it may be more productive to simply pick up the phone and say "hello." Let the emotions enter your consciousness, consider them, and then allow them to disperse like clouds giving way to an approaching airplane.

Painful memories often behave like weeds. Stomping on them might only succeed in deepening their roots. But drenching them with sunlight might cause them to burn out.

Principle 4. Remain humble in success and failure

Charles Darwin once wrote:

Ignorance more frequently begets confidence than does knowledge.

Recent research seems to have confirmed his suspicions. The Dunning-Kruger effect (as coined by social psychologists David Dunning and Justin Kruger) is an oft-cited cognitive bias in which people with a low skill level in a given task tend to overestimate their abilities. Unfortunately, an unskilled man is often blithely unaware of his ineptitude. Or, as the management consultant Martin M. Broadwell would say, the trainee is "not conscious of his own incompetence."

Broadwell famously codified his "four stages of competence" model in an attempt to describe the process of skill attainment. The four stages are:

1. **Unconscious incompetence**: When our subject starts his first day on the job, he is wholly unaware of the degree to which his skill level is lacking.
2. **Conscious incompetence**: After a few days of work, the subject may begin to realize how much he doesn't know yet, and how much he still has to learn.
3. **Conscious competence**: The subject has been training for quite some time now. He can complete the task at hand if he devotes conscious mental effort to it.
4. **Unconscious competence**: The subject has been with the company for a long time. His work is now "second nature" to him. He can perform the task without even thinking about it.

Unfortunately, we often don't know which level of competence we currently reside at. The timid among us tend to guess too low, while the more conceited of us guess too high. But even if you're absolutely sure that you are the best in your field, you are still asked to remain critical of your skills during a Hansei-kai.

The doctrine calls upon us to remain humble in failure as well as in success. During a Hansei-kai, practitioners are not allowed to celebrate a "flawless victory." There is no such thing. Instead, every action has room for improvement, no matter how perfectly it was executed. This mindset is exemplified in this stanza from Toyota's Production System Guide:

Even if a task is completed successfully, Toyota recognizes the need for a hansei-kai "reflection meeting"... [It's] a process that helps to identify failures experienced along the way and create clear plans for future efforts. An inability to identify issues is usually seen as an indication that you did not stretch to meet or exceed expectations, that you were not sufficiently critical or objective in your analysis, or that you

lack modesty and humility. Within the process, no problem is itself a problem.

No matter how much success you have in life, there will always be room for improvement. Hence, there will always be a time for Hansei—an honest and humble appraisal of your efforts and actions.

Principle 5. Don't make the same mistake twice

Noteworthy goal-achievement is only possible if you possess a hunger for self-development. For most people, this hunger wanes quickly once they encounter challenges and setbacks. However, there are others who use their personal failures as learning opportunities. Difficult challenges cause them to be even *more* committed to completing a goal.

The utility of Hansei is not that it will safeguard you from future failures. Instead, you will know that Hansei is working when you manage to decrease the number of times per day that you catch yourself recidivating.

Everyone fails. But not everyone is able to learn from failure and devise an alternate plan of action to avoid making the same mistake again. As the proverb goes:

Fool me once, shame on you; fool me twice, shame on me.

Ch. 3: Intro to Ikigai

What is an Ikigai?

Ikigai is a Japanese term comprised of two words: "iki" and "kai." The first half of the compound ("iki") translates to "life" or "alive." The latter half ("kai") means "benefit" or "effect." So a casual English translation of the term Ikigai might be "that which brings benefit to life." But many other interpretations have been suggested, such as:

- "the thing that gives your life meaning"
- your "true calling"

- your "labor of love"
- or, simply "your passion"

The term is similar to the adopted French phrases "raison d'etre" (your "reason for existence") or "joie de vivre" (your "zest for life").

More colloquially, one's Ikigai is often described as:

My reason to get out of bed in the morning.

This translation is perhaps my favorite because an Ikigai is often one's primary source of intrinsic motivation. You might try gauging the degree to which you have already found your own Ikigai by considering the following question: **"When you wake each morning, how do you feel about the workday that awaits you?"**

- Do you rise from bed with gusto—eager to take on new projects and meet new challenges?
- Or, do you close your eyes in sorrow—sickened by the thought of spending yet another day at the office?

If your answer to this question was more akin to the latter response, then perhaps you haven't found your Ikigai yet.

A brief history of Ikigai

The exact origins of Ikigai are not known. The word can be traced back to Japan's 8th century "Nara period." But most present-day Japanese citizens do not commonly use the term. However, for the residents of Okinawa—a small island located 400 miles south of the Japanese mainland—the word is very important to their culture and personal wellbeing.

Okinawa Island has long piqued the interest of westerners; most recently because it has been labeled a member of the so-called "Blue Zone"—an area whose inhabitants live much longer than the average global lifespan.

Figure 1 - Okinawa is one of five regions listed in Dan Buettner's book "The Blue Zones: Lessons for Living Longer From the People Who've Lived the Longest."

Before the island was westernized, Okinawa had a longer life expectancy than any other Japanese prefecture. Many theories have been proposed to explain the impressive longevity of the inhabitants.

- Some cite their traditional diet which is low in sugar and high in vegetables—especially local Okinawan sweet potatoes.
- Genetics are surely a factor. The Japanese nation holds a top position in every life expectancy list—ranking in first place (with an average lifespan of 84.3 years) on the World Health Organization's 2019 report.
- Still, others have suggested that the Okinawan mindset might be their key to health.

In a popular 2010 TED Talk entitled "How to live to be 100," the New York Times-bestselling author Dan Buettner proposed that Okinawans are able to achieve a long and thriving life due to their "Ikigai." He stated:

In the Okinawan language there is not even a word for retirement. Instead there is one word that imbues your entire life, and that word is "Ikigai." And, roughly

> translated, it means "the reason for which you wake up in the morning." For this 102 year old karate master, his Ikigai was carrying-forth his martial art, for this 100-year-old fisherman, it was continuing to catch fish for his family— three times a week... The Institute on Aging actually gave a questionnaire to...these centenarians, and one of the questions was... "what is your Ikigai?" And they all instantly knew why they woke up in the morning.

After its introduction at TED, the Ikigai concept seemed to go dormant for a few years. Then, in 2014, the English blogger Mark Winn wrote a post on his website TheViewInside.Me in which he combined the Ikigai concept with a self-development Venn Diagram—originally drawn by the Spanish writer Andrés Zuzunaga.

Figure 2 - Andrés Zuzunaga's diagram originally appeared in Spanish. Mark Winn merged an English translation of the diagram with his conception of Ikigai. The resultant merger of the two concepts went viral in 2014.

Winn's blog post (and its associated sketch) went viral shortly after publication—eventually inspiring thousands of Ikigai-related books, blog posts, videos, and articles. Given this curious synergy of an eastern concept with a western diagram, most of the contemporary instruction on Ikigai is highly derivative of the original Japanese philosophy. While Okinawans tend to use the word in reference to social obligations or personal hobbies, western Ikigai pedagogy often focuses on self-development, skill mastery, and entrepreneurship. This east vs. west bifurcation caused a bit of controversy in the late 2010s. Just as religious sects often fracture or deviate from their original source material, so too do self-development methodologies.

In this book, we'll be utilizing the westernized interpretation of Ikigai—which is more applicable to our goal-setting efforts. The term's etymology is not crucial to our discussion. You can call it your "higher purpose," or call it "your true calling," or call it your "reason to get out of bed in the morning," or call it your "Ikigai." The historical origin of the concept is of secondary importance. What is most important is that you discover *your own Ikigai*.

How to choose your Ikigai

Sometimes, people choose their own Ikigai. And sometimes, an Ikigai chooses you. Like the lover whom you were destined to fall for, you may know her at first glance. Or, your admiration might take years to develop. This is why you must remain vigilant in pursuit of your Ikigai—persistently scanning the horizon, ever-ready to sample new curiosities, new hobbies, and new career prospects as they avail themselves to you. The following exercise should help to get you started on this quest.

First, you can think of your Ikigai as being comprised of four parts:

1. **Passion**
2. **Vocation**
3. **Mission**
4. **Profession**

It's best to ponder these four attributes in the form of four questions. Each time you encounter a new career opportunity, ask yourself:

1. Could this be my **Passion**? How much do I love this skill?
2. Could this be my **Vocation**? How good am I (or could be) at this skill?
3. Could this be my **Mission**? How much will this skill benefit the world?

4. Could this be my **Profession**? How likely am I to get paid well for this skill?

The trick lies in identifying which skills you currently have (or are willing to learn), and then rank-ordering these skills based upon these four attributes.

For example, you may enjoy playing video games, and perhaps you're quite good at them. But, while there are some professional video game players in the world, the actual number of people who turn game-playing into a life-long profession is very small. This goes for other commonly admired occupations too—like dancer, musician, singer, athlete, and actor. So, instead of insisting that your Ikigai is: "playing video games," you might consider a more sensible profession like: "becoming a video game developer."

If programming is not your forte, that's ok. Because the game design profession is quite diverse these days, requiring a multitude of talents— like digital artists, sound designers, voice actors, and marketers. So if you're into video games, then any profession in the game industry is worth your consideration and may have the potential to become your Ikigai.

Now, you try it.

If you haven't downloaded my free worksheet yet, follow this link to get it. If you're reading this book on a Kindle or iPad, you can click the link. Paperback readers can type the link into a smartphone or PC.

www.AnthonyRaymond.org/312

Or, if you prefer, just pull out a blank piece of paper and make four columns. Along the top of each column, write the following questions:

1. How much do I love this skill?
2. How good am I (or could be) at this skill?
3. How much will this skill benefit the world?
4. How likely am I to get paid well for this skill?

Now, for each skill or occupation that might have the potential to be your Ikigai, simply assign a number (from 1 to 10) to each of the four columns. The number represents the degree to which you believe you'll be able to satisfy the question.

For example, the first question is, "How much do I love this skill?"

- If you love the skill of, say, "video editing," then write a "10" in the first column.
- If you don't like video editing at all, then give it a "1."
- If you like it a little bit, then give it a number somewhere in the range of "3" to "6."
- And so on...

Complete each of the four questions in the same fashion, and then sum up the results. Keep repeating this exercise for every skill or hobby that you have ever taken an interest in. When you're done, identify the row that has the highest number of points. This one might be your Ikigai.

Do not feel obligated to discover your Ikigai immediately after this exercise is complete. Instead, you'll want to keep this piece of paper in a safe place. Because each time you stumble upon a new career idea, you'll want to redo the exercise—pondering the four questions all over again.

Your answers to these questions will evolve through the years, just as you will. As you grow older, most of the occupations on your list will probably lose their appeal. Eventually, only one or two items will stand the test of time—reliably receiving high marks each time you repeat this exercise. If you find yourself returning to one occupation again and again, perhaps this truly is your Ikigai.

Be wary of a misaligned Ikigai

In completing the above Ikigai discovery exercise, it's pivotal that you try to be as honest with yourself as possible. If you're unable to conduct an objective evaluation of your own skillset, then you may end up with a *misaligned Ikigai.*

To illustrate the importance of this point, consider the contestants on any of the many talent-search reality TV shows like *American Idol, Britain's Got Talent,* or *The Voice.* Week after week, these programs feature people who have *not* managed to discover their true Ikigai.

- Notice how the majority of the contestants are rejected during their first audition.
- Notice the look of shock and despair on their faces when they're told that they are "just not good enough."
- Notice how they (often humorously) storm off the stage, adamantly refusing to believe that they can't sing and insisting that their passion for singing is not misplaced.

Why is this information such a novel revelation to them?

As we sit at home listening to the American Idol auditions, it's usually quite obvious to us all that the majority of these contestants can't sing very well. So why has this epiphany failed to permeate their skull?

The problem is this: most of these contestants have only succeeded in answering the *first* Ikigai question: "What do you love to do?"

They love to sing.

They really, really love to sing.

But just "loving to sing" is not enough. They haven't properly considered the other three questions:

- How good am I (or could be) at this skill?
- How much will this skill benefit the world?
- How likely am I to get paid well for this skill?

The world has plenty of *bad* singers. And the public won't pay to hear a mediocre voice. Most of these people are simply not meant for the music industry. They have selected their Ikigai poorly. They're pursuing a profession that is ill-suited for their innate talents or disposition.

To avoid a similar quagmire, it's best if you pursue an Ikigai that is comprised of all four ingredients.

- You might find your passion in a well-paying profession. But unless you're producing something that the world really needs, you may not feel like your work has much meaning.
- You can have a vocation that pays well. But if you have no interest in the field, then the work can be torturous.
- You might succeed in discovering your mission, and you may indeed have a passion for it. But perhaps you're just not very good at it. Thus, you might forever be stumbling in your career—never really feeling like you're "getting it."

Many of the contestants on American Idol have mistakenly chosen "singing" as their Ikigai. And they would have assigned the number 10 to each of the four questions in our preceding exercise. So don't be like the contestants on American Idol. Instead, it's best if you work to become intimately familiar with your strengths and weaknesses. If you're new to the workforce, don't be afraid to take on many different types of jobs, side hustles, gigs, and internships. Your initial goal should *not* be to just "make money." Instead, try to sample many careers and learn which ones you're best suited for. While you're engaged in each work-related task, take note of which skills you seem to pick up quickly and which jobs you despise doing. Ping your internal mental state and keep asking yourself the same set of questions:

- "Could this be my Passion?"
- "Could this be my Vocation?"
- "Could this be my Mission?"
- "Could this be my Profession?"
- "Could this be my Ikigai?"

Ch. 4: Defeat Procrastination with your Ikigai

Goals require *action* to accomplish. The opposite of action is inaction. So the enemy of goal accomplishment is inactivity. This inactivity is typically the result of a psychological state of apathy, sloth, despair, or fatigue. More generally, the behavior manifested by these emotions falls under the rubric of "procrastination."

We're all introduced to the vice of procrastination shortly after our school days begin. Students are quick to cite *procrastination* as one of their greatest challenges. A 2013 meta-analysis by the German sociologist Katrin B. Klingsieck found that 70% of college students considered themselves to be "procrastinators," and about half perceived it to be a "major life problem."

To better understand the nature of the beast, let's try a narrative:

Consider a day in the life of a typical college student—we'll call him William. During an uneventful Tuesday evening, we spot him sitting quietly on a bus. He's just completed another day of class, and he's making his way across town to his off-campus apartment. Closing his eyes, he envisions himself arriving home, eating a healthy snack, and settling down for a long night of academic pursuits. He has an important biology exam tomorrow and he needs to be ready for it.

William's bus comes to a stop at an intersection near his apartment complex. He leaps through the double doors and walks into the building's lobby. He then takes an elevator up to the third level and spots the familiar door of his tiny apartment. He shoves a key into the twist lock, enters, and then casually tosses his backpack on the kitchen table.

It is at this point in the story when we should start our "procrastination timer." How many minutes will elapse between the moment William arrived home, to the moment he begins studying? The duration of this delicate period will usually dictate the amount of actual *study time* that our subject will succeed in squeezing into his evening.

Recall that when William was sitting on the bus, his plan for the evening was to "eat a healthy snack and settle down for a long night of academic pursuits." But let's consider how these sessions actually tend to play out:

- First, William pours himself a bowl of Frosted Flakes and turns on a nearby TV to watch Sponge Bob reruns while he's eating dinner. His meal should only take ten minutes to complete. But the cartoon is thirty minutes long, and William wants to see it through to the end.
- Once the cartoon is complete, William heads to his bedroom. He starts up his laptop and notices that his favorite YouTuber has put out a new video. It's only ten minutes long, so it wouldn't hurt to watch it.
- Of course, nobody can watch just one YouTube video. So William devours a couple more videos before closing the web browser. This eats up another thirty minutes of study time.
- With his video-watching session finally complete, William realizes that his next-door neighbors have their stereo cranked up to 11—which makes concentration difficult. He wonders if they're having a party tonight and if they'll invite him over.
- As he plops his heavy textbook open on his desk, he notices that he's a bit more tired now than he was an hour ago. His eyelids feel heavy as he leafs through the book's pages.

- As the minutes tick by, the thought of spending an evening digging through a biology book seems more tedious than he had originally estimated. He can hear his neighbors laughing in the adjacent apartment. They sound like they're having a good time. Suddenly, an evening of pizza, beer, and video games seems much more inviting than a night of memorizing biology facts.

And so goes the cascading decline of William's willpower. He meant to study as soon as he walked through the door. But now, our "procrastination timer" has accumulated almost two hours of wasted time. William doesn't feel like doing much of anything anymore. The shifting sands of emotion that comprise his mental state are subject to a phenomenon that researchers call *dynamic inconsistency*.

- When William arrived home, he had the mindset of a conscientious student—ready to pursue his academic interests with great fervor.
- But now, he has the mindset of a gadabout—longing only to relax and socialize.

William's mood is inconsistent with his stated desires. Instead of studying for his exam, his mind envisions alternate activities. He looks at his open biology textbook and understands what he "should be doing right now." But instead of doing it, he fidgets in his chair, stares at the posters on his bedroom wall, plays with his phone, and dreams of a thousand other things that he'd rather be doing right now.

In other words, William is procrastinating.

The preceding scenario is familiar to us all. Anyone who has ever cringed at the thought of spending another hour on a homework assignment is aware of the internal battles that are fought between our ears—the war between "what you should be doing" and "what you'd rather be doing."

- Is it possible to broker a détente between these divergent factions?
- Or, are these two forces forever destined to clash?

- Is there anything we can do to mitigate the deleterious effects of procrastination?

What is Procrastination?

Let's start by describing the problem.

Dr. Piers Steel of the University of Calgary has crafted an excellent definition of our ailment. He states:

To *procrastinate* is to voluntarily delay an intended course of action—despite expecting to be *worse off* for the delay.

The wording is key here and you should take some time to reflect upon this quote; it reveals much about the mental state of the typical procrastinator.

- Most procrastinators already know what they *should* be doing.
- Most procrastinators already believe that their *intended course of action* is superior to the one they're currently on.
- Most procrastinators are keenly aware of the fact that, for every minute they procrastinate, they are only hurting themselves.

Conventional wisdom dictates that procrastination arises because of a lack of time management skills. I.e., if the sufferer were to merely manage his time better, then he would stop procrastinating. However, this approach (while sometimes helpful) fails to address the heart of the issue.

When someone is in the throes of a procrastination session, then introducing them to a "hot new time-management technique" doesn't really help them much. Such tips may increase the efficiency of a person who is already hard at work. But they may not be applicable to someone who is so crippled by procrastination that he can't even get started.

Moreover, it's simply not the case that our subject is procrastinating because of a "lack of time." He has time available to him. He's just not using it to do anything productive. Ironically, it is actually the threat of *insufficient time* (i.e., a looming deadline) that is most effective in terminating a procrastination session. This is why every student discovers the will to study for their final exam on the night before the test.

So, if procrastination doesn't come from a mere "lack of time" then where does it come from?

Let's start by breaking the triggers of procrastination down into four categories:

1. **Distraction** - External stimuli (unrelated to the task at hand) which draws our subject's attention away from his primary objective.
2. **General mental fatigue** - When the brain is depleted of energy, it will summon emotions to prevent the subject from overworking it.
3. **Anxiety** - The general feeling of unease that our subject feels when considering the amount of labor needed to complete his objective. We experience anxiety when pondering a sheet of math problems in the same way we would when preparing to lift a heavy object. Additionally, the subject might feel anxious about the outcome. He might be afraid to fail, afraid to succeed, or he may even think that his actions will lead to momentous life changes (good or bad) that he may be unprepared for.
4. **Negative emotional associations with the task** - The set of negative emotions that emerge because the subject has had a bad experience with the task in the past. His mind is aware of how grueling the work can be, and it doesn't see the immediate value in doing it. So his brain will formulate reasons to avoid putting in the effort.

Of these four triggers, the solutions needed to resolve the first three are fairly straightforward. Much has been written elsewhere about eliminating anxiety, ridding your workstation of distraction, and guarding against mental fatigue. Your brain gets tired after a workout just as your arms and legs do. This is why mental tasks typically seem achievable when you first rise from bed in the morning, and why they seem strenuous when you're nodding off at 11:00 pm. Just as you can't expect your biceps to keep lifting weights all day and night, you can't expect your brain to manifest the same level of willpower throughout every moment of the workday. To mitigate these effects, you can start by utilizing all those clever time management techniques that you've already read about online at websites like Gizmodo, Lifehacker, or WikiHow. Their articles often feature useful brain hacks such as:

- Work on your most difficult tasks in the morning—when your mind is fresh. And do the easier tasks (which don't require as much cognitive effort) later in the day.
- Get eight hours of sleep each night. Consider using blackout curtains to keep your room dark if you have a misaligned sleep schedule.
- Boost your daily energy level via diet and exercise.
- Avoid munching on sugar and carbs before or during a study session.
- Use an hourly calendar to block out distraction-free work times.
- Use the Pomodoro Method to concentrate in 25-minute bursts of attention, followed by a 5-minute break.
- Silence your cellphone and keep it away from your workstation (preferably in another room) so that you're never tempted to reach for it while studying.
- Install software on your PC to limit access to distracting websites during your deep work hours.

All of these tips are great. I myself—being a master procrastinator—have utilized each one.

- I've been using the Pomodoro Method every day for the last eight years. (I'm using it right now to write this book.)

- I have a software app called *Cold Turkey Blocker Pro* installed on my PC to prevent distracting websites from loading.
- And my cell phone spends the first eight hours of each day locked in a plastic bin—the *KSafe Battery-powered Time-Release Lockbox* (aka the best 59 dollars I ever spent).

Figure 3 - The KSafe Lockbox features a time-release lock that can be set to remain closed for several hours each day.

While such tactics are good at resolving the first three triggers of procrastination, we should devote some time to discussing the fourth item in our preceding list of triggers: "negative emotional associations with the task."

Even after you have applied every time-management tip to be found on Lifehacker.com (e.g., after you've eliminated distractions from your PC, after you've defenestrated your cell phone, and after you've found a quiet room to work in), you might *still* have trouble summoning the desire to actually labor through the task at hand. Despite having all your life hacks in place, it may *still* be the case that you just don't *feel* like working.

This is when the *perceived value* of the labor comes into question. When your brain has trouble envisioning the resultant benefit of engaging in a laborious task, then it will utilize negative emotions to prevent you from doing the task. To illustrate this point, let's try a couple thought experiments.

Thought Experiment 1

When we last left our college student, William, he was sitting in his apartment with an open biology textbook on his lap. He knows that he should be studying in preparation for tomorrow's exam, and he has allocated this block of time for the task. But he's not doing it.

He's just sitting there...

He's procrastinating...

Suddenly, space mogul Elon Musk bursts into William's room and tells him that SpaceX has received several communiqués from the future. People of the year 2400 have notified him that William is destined to become the greatest microbiologist of all time. His research will save millions of lives and he will become a household name with a long and credentialed career in academia. But this possible future hinges upon one solitary event—the outcome of tomorrow's biology exam. Failing to get a passing grade will result in a cascade of undesirable decisions which will cause William to drop out of college and join the circus.

Placing a hand on William's shoulder, Elon looks at him with concerned eyes and says, "Please, study hard and ace that test. We're all counting on you." He then hops into an awaiting helicopter and flies away.

Now, let's consider the following questions:

- Do you think it will be easier for William to eschew the temptations that are currently drawing his attention away from studying?
- Do you think he will be less inclined to let video games, student parties, or social media distract him from the task?

- Do you think William is now in a better position to convince his mind and body to put in the long hours of study that will be required to pass tomorrow's test?

Reflect upon those questions while we consider a second thought experiment.

Thought Experiment 2

Now suppose William is again visited by Elon Musk, but the news is less momentous. Elon tells William that SpaceX has invented a device that can make predictions about the future. The machine has determined that there is a 65% chance that William will be changing majors next year—from biology to architecture. Thus, the credits obtained in William's biology class may not be of any value to him at all. Studying for tomorrow's exam might be a waste of William's time.

"Just thought you'd like to know," Elon shouts as he departs in his helicopter.

Alone again in his room, William is left to consider this new tidbit of information. He stares at the long bodies of text in his biology book as waves of doubt and anxiety wash over him. Scratching his chin, he leans back in his chair and thinks, "What's the point of studying this information if there is a 65% chance that it will be completely worthless to me?"

As the minutes tick by, his reservations multiply. Soon, the thought of spending the evening playing video games seems far more appealing than a night spent intensely studying. William throws his pencil down in frustration and spends the next couple of hours moping around his room.

Let's Review

What story elements differed in our above two thought experiments? Why was William able to avoid procrastination in *scenario one* but not in *scenario two*?

- In our first thought experiment, we attached a valuable reward to the outcome of William's labor. Acing tomorrow's test will make him rich, famous, and successful. Additionally, his future medical research will have great benefit to humanity—earning him the admiration of his peers and academic prestige. Given the desirability of each of these lures, William's lower mind was able to readily conjure the willpower needed to study for the test.
- However, in the second scenario, the perceived value of the task was far less certain. There was a 65% chance that William's future academic career would not benefit from the exam's outcome. The toil that he was about to expend on the chore of studying may have been misplaced—having no positive effect on his future life goals. Consequently, William's brain had trouble discerning the value in spending an evening studying, so it prompted him to procrastinate.

Unfortunately, real life is laden with such troublesome probabilities. The realized value of our labor—particularly when it comes to academic pursuits—cannot be forecasted. We just don't know if the information we're learning will ever be very useful to us. So we devise reasons to defer the labor that is required to learn it. Of course, this avoidance strategy applies to other domains too:

- We don't know if we'll like the city we're considering moving to, so we put off calling the realtor.
- We don't know if the girl in our class would ever go on a date with us, so we put off asking for her phone number.
- We don't know if our business proposal will result in praise or mockery, so we put off telling anyone about it.

We just don't know...

The more uncertain we are of the potential benefit of a task, the easier it is for the lower mind to concoct reasons to avoid doing it. Procrastination is your brain's way of telling you that it doesn't see the immediate value in expending the energy that you're asking it to devote to the task at hand. Your lower mind is very good at pursuing short-term pleasures. And very bad at assessing the potential value of long-term goals.

Your conscious mind knows that if you, say, complete medical school, then good things will happen. But your lizard brain doesn't even know what a textbook is, and it doesn't understand why you're spending so many hours staring at the little black lines on its pages. Hence, it will utilize emotional countermeasures in an attempt to incite you to select another course of action. If such ploys are allowed to inflict your consciousness, you might feel compelled to abandon your obligations entirely—replacing them with the pursuit of carnal desires or creature comforts. Additionally, if your mind becomes completely convinced that the action you're engaged in is utterly meaningless, then it will excrete a torrent of negative emotions that will make the task torturous.

To understand this point, let's briefly recount a tale told by the Russian novelist Fyodor Dostoevsky.

Dostoevsky on Career Aspirations

While serving a four-year sentence at the Katorga prison camp in Siberia, Dostoevsky had plenty of time to ponder the hardships of man. Curiously, he noted that he had been sentenced to "four years of hard labor." And yet, the work wasn't actually very difficult. The peasants, he observed, often worked harder than the inmates—assumedly because they were (at least in part) working for themselves, sometimes on their own plot of land.

In observing this dichotomy, Dostoevsky concluded that work is "hardest" when it is meaningless. He wrote:

It once came into my head that if [someone] desired to reduce a man to nothing, to punish him atrociously ... [then one could do so by putting him to work at a task that was completely useless]. Hard labor ... presents no interest to the convict; but it has its utility. The convict makes bricks, digs the earth, builds... [And sometimes] even the prisoner takes an interest in what he is doing. He then wishes to work more skillfully, more advantageously. [However, if the prisoner is forced to] pour water from one vessel into another, or to transport [dirt] from one [hole] to another, [only to dig it up and move it back again], then I am persuaded that, at the end of a few days, the prisoner would strangle himself ... rather than endure such torments.

Such epiphanies reveal why it is so important for each of us to discover our Ikigai (our "true calling"). We must find an occupation that is (in some way) meaningful to ourselves as well as to the community. Work is much easier (and procrastination wanes) when the worker is convinced that his labor will result in genuine value—if not to himself, then to his fellow man (preferably to both).

Unfortunately, many of us are enrolled in college classes or working in dead-end jobs that are not particularly useful to anyone. Often, the motivation to pursue such activities is the result of an external driver.

- Perhaps you only signed up for college because a family member insisted that you do so.
- Perhaps you're only working a soul-crushing corporate job because the pay is good.

If you don't see any genuine value in the fruit of your labor (other than pleasing a parent or a pocketbook), then your mind may exist in a state of perpetual conflict. You will forever be struggling to get your lower brain to follow your orders. You'll have to keep devising pretenses—little lies used to coax yourself into believing that a life of pushing papers across a desk is a life worth living.

This is why an Ikigai is multi-dimensional. We must seek out an occupation that fulfills all *four* of our criteria. Let's list them one last time:

1. Passion - How much do I love this skill?
2. Vocation - How good am I (or could be) at this skill?
3. Mission - How much will this skill benefit the world?
4. Profession - How likely am I to get paid well for this skill?

Unfortunately, most people in the West are blinkered in their quest for happiness. They solely pursue the fourth trait—caring only about how much money they can make.

The management of money will always be an issue in your life, but it must not be the only factor you consider when weighing your life goals. If this is the case, then you may wake one day to find yourself stuck in a job you hate and dreading the notion of spending another day engaged in tasks of meaningless drudgery.

The human willingness to exchange colorless hours of life for money is a curious behavior that lead the Yale anthropologist David Graeber to write his 2018 best-selling book "Bullshit Jobs." Here, Graeber defined a "bullshit job" as:

A form of paid employment that is so completely *pointless*, *unnecessary*, or *pernicious* that even the employee cannot justify its existence.

In the book, Graeber provides several examples of such occupations: lobbyists, corporate lawyers, telemarketers, public relations specialists, door attendants, and middle managers.

We should note that Graeber is quick to distinguish between a "bullshit job" and a "shit job."

- A "shit job" is just a job that sucks. However, the service its practitioners perform might actually be quite valuable. For example, janitors and trash collectors are often said to have "shit jobs" but not "bullshit jobs." If these men and women don't show up to work tomorrow, then we'll all be up to our eyeballs in garbage. Their job, though it might be unpleasant, is far from meaningless.
- A "bullshit job" is (by definition) meaningless. It results in no value to the world except that it provides a salary — sometimes a very large salary — to the person who holds the bullshit job.

Nothing will incite you to procrastinate more than the realization that the work you are about to force your body to do is utterly pointless and devoid of any existential value. People are often at their *worst* when they are coerced into performing a rudimentary cognitive task, all the while knowing that the product of their toil benefits absolutely no one.

A few years ago, I had the opportunity to witness the depths of this mental miasma when I thought it would be fun to learn how to play blackjack. Anyone who has seen the 1988 film "Rainman" or the 2009 film "The Hangover" knows that blackjack is actually a winnable game. The player need only be willing to teach himself to do some quick mental math as the cards are dealt before him.

For most players, card counting is nothing more than a hobby. But to make serious money, professional card counters must spend hundreds of hours sitting at smoky casino tables, performing mental multiplication operations, and hoping to accumulate a tall stack of plastic chips before the pit boss gets too suspicious of their ploy. For some card counters, the pay is decent—sometimes reported at around $80,000 per year. And yet, despite this enviable salary, most card counters don't last very long.

Why?

The writer and professional blackjack player Arnold Snyder blatantly answered this question in the final chapter of his book "A Blackbelt in Blackjack." Here, Snyder wrote:

[If you succeed in becoming a] professional gambler, there is one last problem you will face. You must learn to deal with the existential fear of being a replaceable cog in a machine that produces nothing. Human beings ... have this weighty fixation on doing something important, producing something of value, [and] making a difference [in] the world... [But]...professional gamblers relinquish this human need... Card counters are simply siphoning money from a meaningless cash flow system. They produce nothing, perform no service, entertain no one, and (in the true sense of the word), they are financial parasites to an industry...

The above stanza is a scolding reminder of the peculiarities of human psychology and motivation. And it is especially telling when we consider that it was written by a man who has had great success in blackjack. Yet, while amassing his fortune, he stumbled upon some bitter truths.

- Humans do indeed like to think of themselves as "important."

- We like to think of our work as "valuable."
- We don't like to perceive ourselves as mere "cogs in a machine…siphoning money from a meaningless cash flow system."

As David Graeber would say, professional card counters have a "bullshit job." Or, as I would put it, professional card counters have an "improperly aligned Ikigai."

Human motivation is a bizarre thing. The other mammals seem content once their primal desires are satisfied. But us humans are in pursuit of something more.

Figure 4 - Man has been blessed (or cursed) with the unique ability to question the utility of his own existence.

The behavioral economist Dan Ariely is famous for conducting economics experiments that reveal curious human proclivities. Oddly, when subjects are offered higher rewards for higher levels of productive output, something strange happens; an increase in pay does not always result in an increase in job performance. In describing this phenomenon, Daniel Pink (author of "Drive: The Surprising Truth About What Motivates Us") wrote:

[When the subject's task] involved only mechanical skill, [then monetary] bonuses worked as they would be

expected—the higher the pay, the better [the employee] performance... But once the task called for even 'rudimentary cognitive skill,' [then] a larger reward led to poorer performance. Now, this is strange. A larger reward led to poorer performance? How can that possibly be?

Take a moment to contemplate how bizarre this finding is. When the task requires conceptual thinking, creative effort, and a modicum of cognitive ability, then *increasing* your financial reward might actually have a negative effect on your job performance.

Why this phenomenon occurs is still a mystery. But it seems that financial incentives are secondary to other motivating factors like Autonomy, Mastery, and Purpose.

- **Autonomy** describes our desire to lead a self-directed life—to have the freedom to make choices for our daily activities.
- **Mastery** describes our inner urge to become an expert in a particular skill.
- **Purpose** describes our desire to engage in activities that are beneficial and meaningful—to ourselves, our family, and to our community.

These constituents formulate an intrinsic motivation cocktail—the potion we need to defeat procrastination and silence the childlike pleadings of the lower mind. Once you have imbibed from this cup, you may be surprised at the level of grit that you're capable of manifesting. An angry boss or a looming deadline will not be required to spur you to action. Instead, you'll genuinely want to do the work. Nothing will grind the gears of motivation more vigorously than the belief that the fruit of your labor has real, lasting, and important value—to yourself or others. As the Hungarian-American psychologist and author of "Flow: The Psychology of Optimal Experience" Mihaly Csikszentmihalyi wrote:

It is when we act freely, for the sake of the action itself (rather than for ulterior motives), that we learn to become more than what we were.

Meaning and Passion

If you are one of the fortunate among us who someday succeeds in finding your perfect Ikigai, then congratulations! However, do not be disheartened if you ultimately come to realize that your world does not instantly transform into a paradise on Earth. You're still going to have good days and bad days. There will still be mornings when you'd rather not go into the office. Each successive step up the staircase of mastery can be just as grueling as the previous step. And the more steps you scale, the more work you'll have to devote to the climb. The fruits of your Ikigai might only ripen after years of intense dedication and daily exertion. Mastery usually only comes after we have suffered through the pains of learning our craft. As Mark Z. Danielewski wrote:

Passion has little to do with euphoria and everything to do with patience. It is not about feeling good. It is about endurance. Like patience, passion comes from the same Latin root: "pati." It does not mean "to flow with exuberance." It means "to suffer."

Have you ever met someone on a mission?

Someone who walked with purpose?

Someone on an important quest?

When you do, you might notice that they are quick to cite the many challenges that they have encountered throughout their journey. If you ask them if they "like their job," they might be more apt to describe it as "fulfilling" rather than "fun."

As the American poet Dorothy Parker said:

I hate writing, [but] I love having written.

Innovative people often have a love-hate relationship with their careers. They may genuinely "love their job." But creative output and ingenuity require long hours of intense labor:

- Long hours in an office,
- or in a laboratory,
- or at a typewriter,
- or at a chalkboard,
- or at an easel,
- or at a drafting table,

- or in front of a computer screen.

Finding your Ikigai often entails simultaneously discovering the fount of your greatest inspiration as well as the arena in which your toughest battles will be waged. This is where the *passion* of the process comes into play. The most valuable Ikigais are not mere hobbies; they are quests. Quests worthy of a lifetime of devotion.

As Steven Pressfield wrote in his book *The War of Art*:

To the amateur, the game is his avocation. To the pro it's his vocation. The amateur is a weekend warrior. The professional is there seven days a week.

Even the most talented artisans, researchers, doctors, athletes, engineers, and craftsmen are all still susceptible to the appeal of sloth. But their Ikigai enables them to rise with the sun each morning and labor through another workday.

We can never truly free our minds from the vice of procrastination any more than we can wish away feelings of hunger, lust, or fatigue. Highly productive people must combat the basal desires of the mind each day. This is why Steven Pressfield titled his book "The War of Art." Because productive human effort is no "walk in the park."

It's a war!

A war against yourself.

Every morning is a new battle in which victory is only attained via practiced discipline and an hour-by-hour commitment to a righteous cause.

- So what is your righteous cause?
- What is your "reason to get out of bed in the morning?"
- What is your Ikigai?

In Greek mythology, the Sirens swam in the waters that Ulysses sailed—waiting for the opportunity to lure sailors from ships with their enchanting music. In the same sense, your emotions (doubt, fatigue, boredom, despair, listlessness, and fear) will forever be lurking in your proximity—waiting for an opportunity to convince you to abandon your goals.

- This is why you must devote yourself to a meaningful cause.
- This is why you must sail with purpose.
- This is why you must seek out an Ikigai that is true and righteous.

For, if your quest is righteous, then your mind will summon the tenacity required to circumnavigate life's many hazards, and the resolve needed to resist the seductive songs of the Sirens.

Ch. 5: Intro to Kaizen

When people pursue a new goal, they often start by pledging their commitment to a single colossal objective like:

- "I want to lose 80 pounds by New Year's Eve!"
- Or, "I want to be a millionaire!"

They then pledge their commitment to a work regimen that would require a Herculean effort to achieve. Since most of us do not have the strength and willpower of Hercules, most of us never manage to stick to such commitments for very long. We usually only last a few days before quitting (sometimes only a few hours).

- So why does this happen?
- Why can't we stick to the plan, even when we're convinced that doing so would be in our best interest?
- Why do we fail so often?

Merely vocalizing a vow to attain an objective is the easiest part of the goal-accomplishment process. It doesn't require much effort to devote ourselves to a future goal when we're pledging our commitment from a place of comfort. But, as the process gets underway (as fatigue, hunger, boredom, and anxiety creep in to alter our neurophysiology) then our tenacity wanes and the task begins to lose its appeal.

- Suddenly, the biology textbook starts to look like the riddle of the Sphinx.
- The treadmill in the corner starts to look like a torture device.
- The leftover pastry in the fridge starts to look like a delicacy.
- And that crate of wine in the garage starts to look like an oasis.

Unfortunately, even the most enlightened among us often fail to maintain impressive levels of willpower for very long. The many little disturbances of life chip away at our willingness to stay the course. Most new goals are abandoned soon after they are created. According to a 2007 study by Richard Wiseman of the University of Bristol, 88% of New Year's Resolutions fantastically fail within a few months of the party's conclusion.

Now, with Kaizen, things are different. The "goal setting" mentality is shifted—focusing the mind of the practitioner on a set of objectives that are more readily achievable, and then prompting him to expand upon his performance daily.

To better grasp the meaning of the term, consider that it is comprised of two Japanese words: "Kai" and "Zen." The first word, "Kai" can be interpreted as "change," and "Zen" means "good" or "improve." So a direct translation of "Kaizen" might be "change for the good," "change for the better," or just "improvement."

In one sentence, we might define the methodology this way:

Kaizen is a goal-achievement technique that encourages continuous improvement via daily incremental progress.

To thoroughly understand this concept, it's best if we start at the beginning.

A Brief History of Kaizen

Though Kaizen principles are traditionally associated with Japanese manufacturing, they partially originated in America. During World War II, American companies didn't have the time to develop and test radical manufacturing ideas nor the resources to retool existing factory processes. Instead, they attempted to improve output and efficiency by making small alterations to existing systems. Ideally, these changes would be implemented in just one day—thus requiring minimal factory downtime. Such "continuous improvement" methods proved to be successful, and the process was eventually formalized and packaged with other management curriculum in a course entitled "Training Within Industry" (TWI).

After World War II, The Marshall Plan called for $2.4 billion to be put toward the rebuilding of Japanese industry. American occupation forces brought consultants into Japanese factories to revitalize the wounded Japanese manufacturing economy. In 1951, a training film was produced called "Kaizen eno Yon Dankai" or (in English) "Improvement in Four Steps." This would become the first instance of Kaizen pedagogy to ever be published.

In the years following World War II, the Kaizen methodology continued to evolve thanks to the work of both Japanese and American managers—three of which are listed here:

- The Iowa-born statistician **Dr. William Edwards Deming** made many consulting trips to Japan during reconstruction efforts and was so influential in turning around Japanese industry that he was awarded the *Second Order Medal of the Sacred Treasure* by Emperor Hirohito in 1960. (We'll be referring to Deming's work many times throughout this book.)
- The business consultant **Masaaki Imai** published a management guidebook entitled "Kaizen: The Key to Japan's Competitive Success." He also founded the Kaizen Institute Consulting Group (KICG) with the aim of introducing Kaizen techniques to Western companies.
- **Dr. Jeffrey Liker** (Professor Emeritus of Industrial and Operations Engineering at the University of Michigan) would bring Kaizen into the mainstream when he published his book of "manufacturing ideals" called "The Toyota Way." The book showcased many Kaizen-related principles and described the philosophy and values that dictate the modus operandi of the Toyota Motor Corporation.

Given the stellar success of Japanese industry in the post-World War II years, it's easy to see why the Kaizen philosophy was so quick to leap off the factory floor and into the personal lives of the workers who used it. In recent times, Kaizen has spread throughout the world—enthusiastically applied in both business and self-development pursuits.

Thankfully, Kaizen concepts do not necessarily require the practitioner to adopt the industrial rigor of a factory production line. All of the techniques are quite fungible—able to be applied to even the most domestic of pursuits.

So, how do we learn Kaizen?

Because the development of Kaizen spans multiple decades, countries, and generations, there does not exist one definitive source for the philosophy. Moreover, when a company incorporates Kaizen techniques, they inevitably alter the schema to best suit their own business needs. So one man's Kaizen will differ from that of another.

With that said, I have tried to condense the methodology into six fundamental principles—designed to provide a solid foundation from which you can evolve your own Kaizen style.

The 6 Principles of Kaizen

Kaizen Principle 1: Start working toward your goal immediately, even if your first action is laughably small.

In Kaizen, our first step is to atomize the challenge before us. We do this by asking ourselves one question:

What small step could I take today which may (in the long run) improve my situation?

This initial query is foundational in Kaizen, and we'll be referring to it many times throughout this book. Our aim here is twofold:

- **First**, we want to break our objective down into its smallest constituent parts—identifying the challenges that will be easiest to tackle first.
- **Second**, by surmounting the tiniest hurdles first, we hope to build up psychological momentum. Your lower mind needs to believe that it has the ability to accomplish a smaller goal before it will allow your conscious mind to engage in loftier pursuits.

An initial Kaizen goal might be so tiny and inconsequential that its successful completion could be considered "laughable." That's ok. With Kaizen, we understand that even a tiny action is better than no action at all. For example:

- Instead of choosing to work on nothing today, you might try writing just one paragraph of your novel.
- Instead of staring at the rubbish pile in your garage, you might try spending five minutes cleaning out one section.
- Instead of refusing to exercise at all today, you might try jogging on your treadmill for one minute.

In glancing at our list, it may be difficult to see how such tiny actions could ever amount to anything at all. And initially, they won't. But we're not trying to accomplish all of your life goals in one day. That's impossible. Instead, our first objective is merely to move your mind past the hurdle of "getting started." As Robert Maurer (UCLA professor of behavioral sciences and author of "One Small Step Can Change Your Life") wrote:

Your brain is programmed to resist change. But, by taking small steps, you effectively rewire your nervous system so that it does the following: "unsticks" you from a creative block, bypasses the fight-or-flight response, [and] creates new connections between neurons so that the brain enthusiastically takes over the process of change...

By invoking this incrementalist strategy, we hope to actualize "tiny victories," which will in turn coax the mind into accepting that our efforts are yielding fruit.

This is why the Canadian clinical psychologist Jordan Peterson is famous for helping wayward college students solve their life problems by advising them to "clean your room." In 2017, these three simple words struck a chord with many—at least enough to become a minor internet meme. His intent was to encourage the procrastinating student to get started doing *something*—even if that something seems inconsequently small. Such micro goals (which are typical of initial Kaizen objectives) help to appropriately frame the challenge—prompting the practitioner to opt for action over stagnation.

This first step takes some discipline to achieve, but not as much as you might think. With Kaizen, we hope to muster the tenacity to complete *little actions* in the present, with the eventual goal of pursuing *big gains* in the future. To the lower mind, the successful completion of a minor goal makes the next goal appear all the more doable. When taken in aggregate, this accumulation of tiny daily victories can lead to big life changes.

Figure 5 - University of Toronto professor Stephen Morris knocks down a 100-pound domino using a series of progressively lighter dominos—the first one is smaller than a Tic Tac.

"Touching the Void"

The elusive utility of this philosophy was nicely exemplified in the 1988 novel "Touching the Void" by the English mountaineer Joe Simpson. While climbing Siula Grande in the Andes Mountains of Peru, Simpson tragically broke his leg and lost his climbing partner. Suffering from intense pain and pelted by a blinding snowstorm, Simpson could do little more than carefully hobble across the perilous terrain. In an effort to keep himself motivated, he wrote:

...it occurred to me, that I should set definite targets. I started to look at things and say, "If I can get to that crevasse over there in 20 minutes, that's what I'm going to do"... If I got there in 18 minutes, I was hysterically happy. And if I got there in 22 minutes, I was upset to the point of tears. It became almost obsessive. I'd look at [another] rock, and [say], "Right, I'll get there in 20 minutes." Once I decided to go *that* distance in 20 minutes, I bloody well was going to do it. [This technique] would help me, because I'd get halfway through the distance and I'd be in [so much pain that] I couldn't bear the thought of getting up and falling on [my leg] again. But I'd look at the time and think, "I've got to get there."

By pledging his commitment to the completion of a thousand tiny goals, Joe Simpson pulled himself down the west face of Siula Grande and back to basecamp. Each mile of the journey stretched across sharp rocks, crags, and gravel. He traversed the entire distance while tending to a broken leg and combating frostbite and dehydration. He survived, arriving at basecamp on the evening before his friend Simon Yates was due to hike out.

When faced with such a dire situation, most people would have given up hope. But Simpson broke the immense challenge down into a thousand tiny objectives—each with a time horizon of about twenty minutes. While he was completing these mini-deadlines, he narrowly focused his mind on the immediate task—not on the enormity of the impossible challenge that lay before him.

The success of Joe Simpson's strategy is illustrative of the power of Kaizen.

- With Kaizen, we identify the problem, break it down into small achievable goals, and we put one foot in front of the other— progressing steadily forward in pursuit of our prime objective.
- With Kaizen, we don't spend too much time worrying about the vastness of the challenge that lies before us. Instead, the next step itself is the only challenge we're concerned with.

Of course, there is a time and a place for long-term planning exercises. But if we sit in awe of lofty goals, then we may become blind to the immediate actions that could be accomplished in the here and now. Kaizen practitioners are asked to temporarily put aside the long-term planning apparatus of the mind, and instead focus on proximal goals that could be accomplished now. Once you learn to focus your mind on the task at hand, then the quest that lies before you may not look so challenging.

As Lao Tzu wrote:

A journey of a thousand miles begins with a single step.

Kaizen Principle 2: Use a "Continuous Improvement Process" (CIP)

Recall that Kaizen was originally developed to help workers troubleshoot issues and improve efficiency on the factory floor. To formalize this process, they often utilized a "Shewhart Cycle"—an iterative process of problem-solving devised by the American statistician Walter Shewhart and popularized by Shewhart's protégée Edwards Deming. These days, the method goes by several names and exists in many forms—all of which vary slightly depending on the characteristics of the industry in which it is utilized. For our purposes here, we'll be using the "OPDCA" version— which calls upon the practitioner to employ a continuous five-stage process in which he is to: "Observe, Plan, Do, Check, and Adjust."

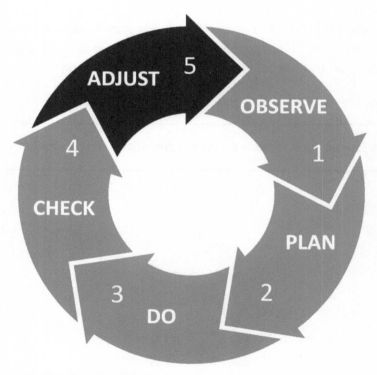

Figure 6 - The OPDCA cycle (also called a "Shewhart Cycle" or "Deming Wheel") prompts the practitioner to solve problems using a continuous iterative process.

We'll discuss each letter of the acronym now.

Step 1: "Observe"

Whenever we encounter a challenging situation, our first task in the OPDCA process is to simply "observe." On the factory floor, engineers and line workers were asked to identify and take note of any problem areas in their workflow. Of course, you don't need to own a factory to find problems that need addressing in life. Perhaps your problem is weight loss, tardiness, or financial planning. Either way, the OPDCA method can help.

Merely observing a problem's cause and effect can be more difficult than it sounds. Consider this passage from Arthur Conan Doyle's Sherlock Holmes short story "A Scandal in Bohemia:"

"When I hear you give your reasons," [Watson] remarked, "the thing always appears to me to be so ridiculously simple that I could easily do it myself, though at each successive instance of your reasoning, I am baffled until you explain your process. And yet I believe that my eyes are as good as yours."

"Quite so," [Holmes] answered... "You see, but you do not observe."

Cataloging your detrimental behaviors (taking note of your own shortcomings) requires a level of honest critique that many are unwilling to engage in, or may not have the capacity to perceive. Just as Watson had to defer to Holmes's superior observational skills, so too must we be open to critique and criticism from others—especially those who have our best interests in mind.

Step 2: "Plan"

The planning phase of the OPDCA cycle calls upon us to devise a process to improve our situation. Of course, we can never be sure that the strategy we're about to execute will produce results that are superior to our current course of action. But that's ok. Remember, Kaizen was initially developed to allow factory workers to attempt small improvements to a process, given the limited resources of the pre-war economy. Suggested alterations were kept small so that, if the gambit failed, at least the attempt wasn't too costly. If our ploy doesn't work out, tragedy will not befall us. Instead, a failed plan is just an opportunity to learn, reevaluate our circumstances, and try again.

Step 3: "Do"

The "do" phase is when the OPDCA practitioner executes the plan. An essential part of this step is the collection of data—which should be (in some fashion) safely logged away for evaluation in Step 4. Your data collection efforts don't have to come in the form of a data-heavy statistical analysis of each action you perform. Instead, it may be as simple as counting calories, logging the number of customers you succeeded in contacting, or recording the number of hours you spend studying for your exams.

Step 4: "Check"

In this step, we analyze the data we collected in the previous step. Here, our intent is to evaluate the extent to which our actual progress varies from our anticipated result. For example, if you aimed to study for two hours per day last week, but only managed to eke out fifteen minutes, then a discrepancy of this size would be something to note.

Step 5: "Adjust"

Finally, in the "adjust" phase, the observations and data points that were collected in the previous steps are finally analyzed. If the desired outcome did not meet the expected outcome, then a hypothesis is formulated in an attempt to identify the root cause of the problem. Changes are then suggested to improve the issue or to prevent the undesirable situation from reoccurring. Once the changes are implemented, the practitioner returns to Step 1 of the OPDCA cycle (the "Observe" phase), and the process of improvement repeats indefinitely. This is why we call it a "Continuous

Improvement Process." Because we can always do better. The wheels of *personal improvement* must never stop spinning.

Kaizen Principle 3: Interpret success and failure correctly

In glancing at the steps in our preceding OPDCA cycle, readers might note that the process looks similar to other familiar problem-solving techniques. You might recall sitting in your high school science class and listening to your teacher explain *The Scientific Method*:

1. Ask a question
2. Form a hypothesis
3. Conduct an experiment
4. Analyze your data
5. Report on your conclusions

These steps are comparable to those seen in the "Observe-Plan-Do-Check-Adjust" method described above. And similar methodologies can be found throughout antiquity. You are, of course, free to develop your own system of inductive reasoning and tailor it to your specific needs. The steps you elect to include in your empirical process are secondary to the framing of the resultant outcome.

In a traditional goal-setting model, a solitary failure often marks the dramatic demise of the practitioner's efforts. For example, he might set out to only consume 1800 calories a day until reaching his target bodyweight. But, after discovering that he ate too many calories on Friday night, he might give up in exasperation and declare, "I have failed! My diet is over!"

Of course, this is *not* how we interpret failure with Kaizen. In our OPDCA checklist, there is no item labeled "failure." Instead, we pledge to stick to the process indefinitely, regardless of the outcome.

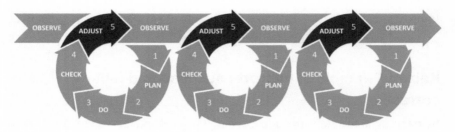

Figure 7 - The OPDCA cycle repeats indefinitely despite the outcome.

The mindset that is cultivated via this framing is essential to the success of the process. Recall how Thomas Edison famously recounted his many failed attempts to invent the lightbulb stating:

I have not failed. I've just found 10,000 ways that won't work.

This is the sort of outlook we must adopt as practitioners of Kaizen. A setback is not a reason to quit. Instead, it's just a data point to be evaluated during our adjustment phase. Your ability to tolerate life's many challenges is in large part dependent upon your ability to properly frame them. You must learn to see obstacles as *opportunities for learning*, rather than as *excuses for capitulation*.

Additionally, just as we are to interpret *failure* as a motivator to press on and keep trying, so too must we view *success* in a similar light.

- In Kaizen, there is no such thing as "good enough."
- We are never permitted to be "set in our ways."
- That old line your grandma used to say, "If it ain't broke, don't fix it," is antithetical to this methodology.

Instead, with Kaizen, we are vigilant to rectify the little inefficiencies of our lives in whatever form they manifest. While we will never achieve perfection, there is great value to be garnered in our devotion to its continual pursuit.

The UK's *Institute of Quality Assurance* defines "continuous improvement" as:

> **...a gradual never-ending change which is...focused on increasing the effectiveness [or the] efficiency of an organization... Put simply, it means "getting better all the time."**

Like corporations, human beings like to see themselves as "getting better all the time" too. With Kaizen, this is of course exactly what we aim to do. We strive to be better. We seek an interminable state of incremental progress—forever improving upon our health, wealth, and relationship goals. Ideally, our wheels of progress will be perpetually spinning—progressing steadily up the steep incline of self-improvement every day.

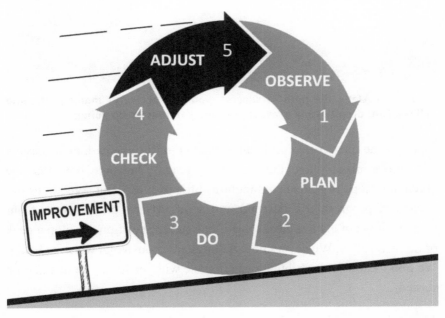

Figure 8 - The goal of the OPDCA cycle is to help us continually progress toward whatever goal we choose.

Of course, any rise to the top will undoubtedly be met with occasional falls. We will inevitably encounter a series of discouraging blunders that prompt us to entertain thoughts of giving up. But, with Kaizen, we understand that some perspective is needed here. The Kaizen process never promised us that every action we engage in will succeed. On the contrary, the majority of actions undertaken in the development of a complicated process will probably result in failure. But it is only when we commit to "keep trying" that we arrive at the realization of the nature of our plight.

Figure 9 - Along the path of success, you will arrive at many peaks and valleys. But, despite your present position, you must keep going.

Examine the many peaks and valleys that comprise the path of success in our above image. Note the variety of crags. On some breadths, the ascending slope is gradual and requires little exertion. But sometimes our wheels of progress will descend into a rut. At any given stage of our journey, it is not always clear to us if our current position sits atop a peak or lies in a valley. We never know if things are about to get worse or better. We don't know if our tribulations are done with, or if they're just getting started.

Alas, this epistemic quandary is a result of the limitations of the human experience.

- We can't predict the future.

- The present is difficult to quantify.
- And our interpretation of the past is notoriously error-prone.

The best we can do is choose to keep progressing forward. Once we pledge to forever keep the wheels of progress spinning, then any undesirable situation in which we find ourselves is necessarily the result of circumstances that are merely transitory. It is only after we commit to the process of *continuous improvement* itself, that *continuous improvement* will be the inevitable outcome of our efforts.

Kaizen Principle 4: Use the "Five Whys" technique to identify a problem's root cause

Originally developed by the founder of Toyota Motor Corporation, Sakichi Toyoda (1867-1930), the "Five Whys" technique prompts the subject to ask a series of questions in an attempt to identify the root cause of a dilemma.

Figure 10 - Sakichi Toyoda was a Japanese industrialist and founder of the Toyoda family of companies. His son, Kiichiro Toyoda, would later establish Toyota Motor Corporation.

For example, suppose a habitually tardy student is considering all of the potential reasons that cause her to miss class. Her Five Whys session might look like this:

"My problem is that I'm always late for class."

1. **Why?** - Because it took too long to walk across the college campus and arrive at my classroom on time.
2. **Why?** - Because I missed the morning bus.
3. **Why?** - Because I wasn't waiting at the bus stop when it arrived.
4. **Why?** - Because I didn't leave my house early enough to make it to the bus stop on time.
5. **Why?** - Because I stayed in bed too long and didn't have enough time to get dressed and eat breakfast.

The goal of this method is to arrive at a final response that is most indicative of the problem's root cause. In our preceding example, the reason why the student was late for school had little to do with the size of her college campus nor the inefficiencies of public transportation. She was late because she stayed in bed too long and didn't have enough time to complete her morning routine.

As we discussed in Chapter 2 (Intro to Hansei), introspective exercises—like the Five Whys method—work best when the practitioner is as honest with themselves as possible. The ability to troubleshoot life problems with an objective eye is a valuable skill to have—applicable in many domains and useful for sussing out the points of friction that hinder our goal accomplishment efforts.

Kaizen Principle 5: Your actions should be daily, not weekly.

In 2007, the tech blog *Lifehacker* published an article by Brad Isaac in which he described a goal-setting trick that Jerry Seinfeld taught him. Isaac was attending an open mic night at a comedy club and had the opportunity to ask Seinfeld if he had any tips for a young comic. In describing the encounter, he wrote:

[Seinfeld] said the way to be a better comic was to create better jokes. And the way to create better jokes was to write every day. He told me to get a big wall calendar that has [an entire] year on one page... The next step was to get a big red magic marker. [Then] for each day that I do my task of writing, I get to put a big red X over that day. After a few days, you'll have a chain. Just keep at it and the chain will grow longer every day. You'll like seeing that chain, especially when you get a few weeks under your belt. Your only job is to *not* break the chain. "Don't break the chain!"

This simple tidbit of advice enjoyed a burst of viral fame shortly after the Lifehacker article was published. It even inspired a cottage industry of Seinfeld-inspired calendars and day planners.

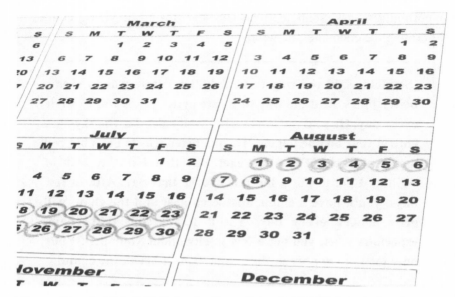

Figure 11 - A "Seinfeld Calendar" consists of all 365 days printed on one page. The practitioner commits to doing one activity each day. A red X marks the successful completion of the task.

Seinfeld's trick is reliant upon the same psychological forces that power Kaizen. The subject is asked to commit to incremental progress—performing a modest task each day of the week without interruption. The level of stick-to-itiveness required to complete such a goal does not seem very impressive at first glance. After all, it's not too difficult to write down a couple jokes every afternoon. Anyone could do it. Right?

But it's only after you've tried (and failed) to maintain a similar self-improvement habit for a month, that you realize how very difficult such challenges can be. The trivialities of life will be forever ready to prevent you from completing even the simplest daily life goal. This is why Seinfeld was so adamant about his rule:

"Don't break the chain!"

By pledging a commitment to perform the task *daily* (not "every other day" and definitely not "weekly"), we can better capitalize upon the mind's predilection for ritual and routine. Ironically, a task might actually seem easier to you if you execute it every day instead of, say, every Tuesday and Thursday. Such is the power of habit.

James Clear, author of the New York Times best-selling book *Atomic Habits*, described the Seinfeld method this way:

Don't break the chain on your workouts and you'll find that you get fit rather quickly.

Don't break the chain in your business and you'll find that results come much faster.

Don't break the chain in your artistic pursuits and you'll find that you will produce creative work on a regular basis.

So often, we assume that excellence requires a monumental effort and that our lofty goals demand incredible doses of willpower and motivation. But really, all we need is dedication to small, manageable tasks.

Mastery follows consistency.

Kaizen Principle 6: Measure your results ritualistically

In Kaizen Principle 2 we described how data collection is an important part of the OPDCA cycle. Recall that Kaizen was initially developed for the factory floor—where every widget was accounted for and the efficiency of every task was scrutinized.

Of course, you are not required to adopt such a statistically rigorous approach to your personal goal-attainment efforts. Nor should you be investing in goal-tracking software, pedometers, or iPhone apps. Such devices have their place. But, especially in the early days of your Kaizen training, it's usually best to keep things simple.

- Record your body weight with a bath scale each morning.
- Count the number of calories you consume each day.
- Log the number of hours you spend practicing the violin.
- Time your running speed with a stopwatch.
- Calculate the number of words you've added to your novel.
- Or just use Seinfeld's method, and draw a red X each time you complete your task for the day.

The logging methods and metrics you choose are of secondary concern. What's pivotal is that you start logging *something* each day. Find a method that works for you and get your mind and body accustomed to the ritual of daily tracking.

Forcing yourself to merely keep a record of your progress will cause the task to remain persistent in your mind. If the evening draws near and you haven't completed your goal for the day, then your brain will punish you with negative emotions. Alternatively, if you *do* manage to successfully fulfill your daily obligation, then you'll experience a burst of pride as you log yet another day of incremental progress.

Additionally, maintaining consistent records helps to keep us honest. The human brain has a natural tendency to conflate any variable that has not been written in stone. This is why the size of the trout gets bigger every time your Uncle Ricky tells his favorite fishing story. Data logging helps to counteract this phenomenon and forces us to remain objective when evaluating our past performance. As Edwards Deming wrote:

In God we trust, all others must bring data.

"Jeet Kune Do"

If you take a moment to wade through the sea of Kaizen literature on offer, you'll find many books, videos, blogs, and websites that feature their own set of "timeless Kaizen principles." But as you flip through this material, you'll be quick to note the degree to which these sources diverge.

As with so many other concepts in Asian philosophy, different people come away with vastly different interpretations. There are no hard and fast rules here. And nobody is going to criticize you for invoking your own personal flavor of Kaizen. It's ok to adopt a "Jeet Kune Do" approach to the curriculum.

"Jeet Kune Do" (aka "Way of the Intercepting Fist") is the name of Bruce Lee's personal style of martial arts. It is commonly referred to as a "formless form" of Chinese Kung Fu—not reliant upon any specific style or rigid technique.

There is no central Kaizen authority. Just as each corporation adopts a different set of workflow procedures for their production line, so too are you free to select the Kaizen techniques that are best suited for your own lifestyle and goals.

There is no need to rush the process. Instead, incorporate Kaizen into your mode of living gradually—giving it time to mature and evolve just as you do. Or, as Bruce Lee wrote:

Don't get set into one form... [Instead,] adapt it... build your own, and let it grow...

Figure 12 - This Statue of Bruce Lee, by sculptor Cao Chong-en, stands in the Yau Tsim Mong District in Hong Kong.

Ch. 6: Your first step with Kaizen

In the previous chapter, we discussed how our adventures with Kaizen always start with one question:

What small step could I take today which may (in the long run) improve my situation?

When facing a difficult challenge, it is natural for people to experience anxiety. Often, we already know what we *should be doing* to pursue our objectives. But we fail to get the process started. Kaizen helps to focus the subject's attention on the proximate steps that he could be taking *right now*. This framing helps to prevent his mind from becoming awestruck by the immensity of the obstacle that lies before him.

However, while this paradigm can be effective in atomizing the process, the subject may still have other reservations which are preventing him from taking action. In this chapter, we'll consider four other inquiries which might help to put you in the proper goal-accomplishment mindset.

Question 1: What is holding you back?

Often, the most difficult part of the goal-attainment process does not hinge upon your willingness to change yourself. Instead, the process relies upon your willingness to change your *environment*. If prompted, you could probably identify several negative influences in your environment which are currently hindering your development.

- Are your neighbors partying at all hours of the night?
- Did you spend more time in the corner bar last week than you'd like to admit?
- Are you stuck in a one-horse town?
- Are your evenings spent playing video games with your roommate?
- Does your neighborhood have a crime problem?
- Does your car window get smashed once a month?
- Are you too tired to pursue your side projects after your long evening commute?

When considered one by one, such annoyances might seem inconsequential. But their cumulative effect can be detrimental to your life goals. Often, the best way to mitigate such disturbances is to simply remove yourself from the environment in which they occur. For many, this is easier said than done. Financial circumstances or existing familial obligations may prevent you from flying too far from the nest. Your wings may even be clipped by those closest to you.

- Do you have a parent who insists on plotting your academic career?
- Does your grandmother keep filling your plate with cookies—regardless of your struggles with weight gain?
- Do your siblings laugh at you when they see your nose in a book?

Accomplishing your life goals often means telling friends and family that you hear an alternate calling in life. When your ship is preparing to sail, there will soon come a time when you'll have to decide to hop on board and flee the safe harbor that you call home.

In Scandinavian folklore, the Kraken was a giant squid-like monster that terrorized merchant sailors in the waters of the North Atlantic. A ship might be sailing smoothly along its way. But if the Kraken's long tentacles managed to grab hold of its mast, then all hope was lost. The ship would be pulled down to the depths of the sea—never to be seen again.

The voyage of our life is vulnerable to similarly veiled threats. We may be ready to set sail in pursuit of our dreams. But if we allow ourselves to be held back by the creatures of the deep, then our vessel will fail to reach the blue water; the grand adventure of our lives will amount to nothing more than a fish story.

Like a night watchman scanning the horizon (intent on keeping his ship out of harm's way), so too must we remain on the lookout for the goal-destroyers that lurk around us—the deadweight that prevents us from achieving our dreams. Such nefarious creatures will always be in your proximity. Their tentacles will forever be reaching for you—intent on pulling you down to their level, intent on holding you back.

So what's holding you back?

Figure 13 - The Kraken devours a ship. Pen sketch by the French naturalist Pierre Denys de Montfort (1801).

Question 2: Are you motivated enough to start building good habits today?

The key to understanding why humans have so much trouble building good habits or committing to long-term goals lies in first understanding the limitations of the human mind. The lower mind is very good at evaluating the pros and cons of immediate muscle maneuvers. E.g.:

"If I walk to the kitchen, then I can eat a cookie."

In such circumstances, it is easy for the mind to muster the motivation to perform the work (walk to the kitchen) to get the reward (a cookie). However, when it comes to more complex pursuits, the payoff is rarely so conspicuous. Impressive human endeavors are usually only accomplished following years of dedicated labor. But the mind has trouble invoking such reflexive motivating forces when the outlook for a future reward is dim. It is difficult for us to envisage how the execution of small daily habits could possibly result in substantial future gains.

As a thought experiment, try to imagine how different life would be if we all owned a special television that was capable of displaying imagery from the future. Specifically, suppose the screen could show us the result of sticking to a daily habit for a decade or two. For example:

- A lanky man who considered adopting a weight-training regimen could view what his future physique would look like after ten years of nightly workouts.
- A teenager who had recently taken up smoking with his friends could observe the deleterious health effects of succumbing to nicotine addiction.
- A boy learning to play the cello could hear what he would sound like if he were to practice every day until his 30th birthday.

Such a glimpse into the future could act as a powerful motivating force—able to remove any ambiguity about the potential value of executing a daily habit.

Alas, such a device does not exist. The typical human planning horizon rarely extends beyond a week or two. After that, things get fuzzy. In our attempt to quantify the benefits of adopting new habits, all we can do is guess about potential future gains. Calculating such forecasts is difficult, especially when you don't have many victories under your belt and you lack the experience needed to foresee the value of any given course of action.

This is why, with Kaizen, we start our journey with tiny and immediate steps. Each mile traversed is a little victory in which your mind has the opportunity to acclimate to the process of goal attainment. As you accumulate trophies, your mind will grow more tolerant of a broader planning horizon, and more apt to accept bouts of delayed gratification. Such mental tunings are necessary for the accomplishment of long-term goals and impressive feats.

Question 3: What challenging obstacles have you already overcome in your life?

In Chapter 2, we discussed the importance of Hansei ("honest self-reflection") and the utility of remaining critical of your own abilities. Striving for objectivity regarding your strengths and weaknesses will aid in avoiding complacency and prevent you from straying from the path of continuous improvement. However, while you are wise to remain humble about your skillset, you should take an occasional moment to acknowledge your past victories.

Everyone has overcome a challenge of some size. Everyone has faced a scuffle in which they came out on top. Maintaining a log of such triumphs can be invaluable on the days when the spirits of intrinsic motivation are not so easily conjured, or when the impediments before you appear insurmountable.

It's easy to stand awestruck at the difficult trial that lies before you. But it's even easier to forget the many defeated obstacles that lie toppled behind you—silently laid out atop the ground that you have already won.

Figure 14 - It's easy to forget how much you have learned and how far you have come.

Question 4: How would you define an "ideal workday?"

When you wake each morning, you should have a template in mind which describes what an "ideal workday" looks like. In outlining such a day, it's important to avoid confusing an "ideal workday" with a "successful day" or a "lucky day"—such as a day when your stocks go up in value or when you receive a new promotion. Such events should be celebrated. But an ideal workday is not dependent upon the whims of fortune or serendipity. Instead, we define it this way:

An ideal workday is one in which you complete all of the objectives that are under your control.

For example, if you had planned to work for six uninterrupted hours on a new project, and you actually succeed in doing so, then this accomplishment fulfills the criteria for an ideal workday. However, if you allowed your brain to entertain interruptions then your productive output probably waned.

- Did you stop your workflow to answer emails?
- Did you stop your workflow to check your stocks?
- Did you stop your workflow to chat with colleagues?

Each one of these events is under your control. You could have chosen to stick to the original plan (to spend six hours on your new project), but you failed to do so.

Throughout the day, we all rack up hundreds of such failures:

- Were you supposed to study for three hours but spent most of that time texting your girlfriend? *That's a fail.*
- Did you promise yourself to avoid fighting with your neighbor over his protruding shrubbery, but instead allowed his malfeasance to get to you? *That's a fail.*
- Were you supposed to hit the gym after dinner but instead elected to watch your favorite show on Netflix? *That's a fail.*

In a typical workday, even the most enlightened among us will fail constantly. And that's okay. We're human after all. Our productive efforts will forever be susceptible to the volatility of our health and fortune. Minor emergencies (and sometimes major ones) will pry us from our desks— demanding our attention and ruining our carefully planned schedules.

This is why we avoid assessing our efforts based on the unruly circumstances of the day. Instead, we begin each workday with the intent of completing the few tasks that we are capable of controlling. And, at the conclusion of each workday, we should be able to look back upon what we have accomplished and measure the degree to which our *actual day* varied from our *ideal day*. While this margin can never be eliminated, we make an hour-by-hour pledge to keep our error rate as low as possible.

Ch. 7: Two Common Kaizen Objections

When first introduced to Kaizen, students are often quick to mention two concerns:

- First, they refuse to believe that little daily actions could ever amount to anything substantial.
- Second, they posit that Kaizen is just an excuse to do the smallest amount of work possible. After all, if we're only required to set "tiny goals," then "tiny goals" are the only type of goal we shall pursue.

In this chapter, we'll address both of these objections.

Objection 1: "Little actions can't possibly add up to much, can they?"

There's a famous self-help dictum that states:

Most people overestimate what they can do in one year and underestimate what they can do in ten years.

This quote is exemplative of one of man's most unfortunate cognitive limitations. It is very difficult for the mind to consider the results of a set of tiny actions and then to extrapolate upon this information in an attempt to calculate the net result after a decade of similar labor.

Recall the initial question that we are to ask ourselves before initiating a Kaizen exercise:

What small step could I take today which may (in the long run) improve my situation?

When people are told to pursue their goals by first selecting a task that is laughably small, they often consider the initial request to be perplexing. Merely completing a small task seems futile when the primary goal is so large. It can be difficult to foresee how tiny actions could ever result in impressive gains. But this reaction is the result of two misunderstandings:

- **First**, remember, with Kaizen, our objective only starts small. But it doesn't remain small. As stated in previous chapters, the diminutive size of the initial task is aimed at encouraging the practitioner to build up psychological momentum—to get the gears in motion and to get the subject on his feet and working. However, as the days progress, he will be adding increasingly more laborious tasks to his workload.
- **Second**, this reaction fails to appreciate the value of consistency when it comes to lengthy human endeavors. Rome wasn't built in a day. It was built by people who had the tenacity to show up to work every day for generations. Its grand structures were formed by the accumulation of a million little bricks. Moving a single brick into position is not very impressive. But, if the action is repeated a million times, then an empire is formed.

To better appreciate this phenomenon, consider the following exercise. Suppose you were to open a Microsoft Word document (with the default font and paper settings) and type out 2,000 words. This is a modest sum that would fill up about three pages, as evidenced by the below screenshot.

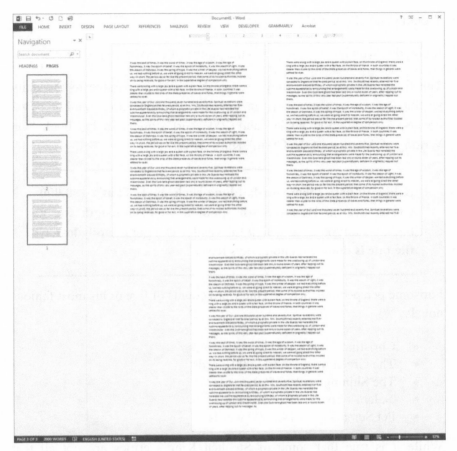

Figure 15 - In this screenshot of Microsoft Word, a 2000-word document requires just three pages.

In glancing at our image, you should note how unimpressive this volume of output is. Even if you're not a writer, it's likely that, at some point in your life, you've stayed up late one night and pounded out a lengthy business proposal, a treatise on the Fall of Rome, or a book report on Peter Rabbit. Thus, the prospect of typing a measly three pages of content probably doesn't seem very impressive to you.

Now, suppose I were to tell you that if you managed to type these three pages each day, then your output would match that of one of the world's most financially successful and prolific writers.

Would you believe me?

If not, then you have yet to grasp the power of *consistency + time*.

The three pages in our above screenshot are comparable to the daily writing output of the American novelist Stephen King—author of 61 novels, 5 non-fiction books, and 200 short stories. In his book "On Writing: A Memoir of the Craft," King states:

> **[I like to get] 2,000 words [done each day]. That's 180,000 words over a three-month span, a goodish length for a book—something in which the reader can get happily lost, if the tale is done well and stays fresh.**

For some perspective, here are the word counts of five of his most famous novels:

- Christine — 189,900 words
- The Green Mile — 177,000 words
- The Shining — 165,500 words
- 'Salem's Lot — 152,200 words
- Pet Sematary — 142,600 words

While it is true that some of Stephen King's critics are not all that impressed with the quality of his work, *none* would say that Stephen King is not prolific. In the proceeding image, we have placed a selection of his book covers so that you can get an idea of the size of the Stephen King bibliography.

Figure 16 - A selection of Stephen King's published works.

This image reveals a striking visual representation of the power of consistency. Difficult human undertakings are often accomplished by a commitment to generate daily output over an extended period of time. Many fortuitous opportunities sit abandoned, not because the task was necessarily difficult, but because the person doing the task didn't have the tenacity to keep at it each day. This is why, with Kaizen, we have stressed the need for a commitment to *daily* progress. Because we understand that *big rewards* usually follow the accumulation of a million tiny victories.

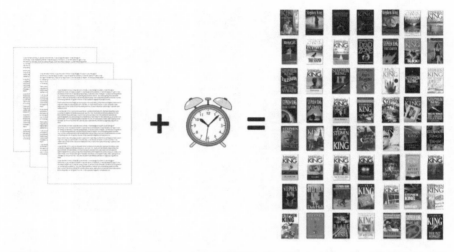

Figure 17 - Writing just three pages (2,000 words) per day, multiplied by 50 years, equals the entire Stephen King library.

Objection 2: "With Kaizen, I only have to do the absolute minimum amount of work each day, right?"

A second objection comes from those who would use Kaizen as an excuse to do the absolute minimal amount of work each day. "After all," they might say, "if I merely show up consistently and get my hours in, then I have fulfilled my daily Kaizen objective, right?" But, this retort negates the very purpose of Kaizen's existence. Remember, our goal with Kaizen is "continual improvement," not "continual homeostasis." If you don't approach each day with the intent of making your present situation incrementally better, then you're not practicing Kaizen. Moreover, merely "showing up" or "putting in your hours" is not sufficient for growth. At each threshold in your development, the effort required for *further* improvement will increase.

To understand this point, consider the work of the Swedish psychologist Anders Ericsson and his so-called "10,000 hour rule." Malcolm Gladwell popularized this rule in his New York Times best-selling book "Outliers: The Story of Success." Here, it is conjectured that mastery of a skill typically comes following 10,000 hours of practice. Hence, if the subject was to merely "get his 10,000 hours in" then he could expect to become a master of his craft.

The problem with this rule is that nobody can agree on the amount of effort required to constitute a single "hour of practice." Not all practice sessions are created equal. It is quite common for a subject to achieve an "acceptable" skill level, and then to halt his forward progression. Despite adding ever more hours of practice time, he fails to achieve additional milestones.

Ericsson notes that medical doctors who have been practicing for 20 years can become complacent if they perceive their job skills to be "good enough"—i.e., sufficient to get them through the workday. When tested, these doctors performed about as well as incoming doctors who had only been practicing for 5 years.

To explain this phenomenon, Ericson distinguishes between "naive practice" and "deliberate practice."

- **"Naive practice"** is what we do when we merely "show up" to work. Some minuscule amount of learning is happening when we start our morning office routine or when we participate in a casual racquetball game with friends. But typically, our skill level does not progress when we aren't challenged to achieve a loftier goal.

- **"Deliberate practice"** occurs when the practitioner is forced to get out of his comfort zone—called upon to display a level of mastery that he has not been capable of in the past. E.g., when a new and complicated piece of music is placed in front of a violinist, or when the hurdles are raised an inch higher at a track meet. During such moments, the practitioner's current skillset is stretched. His mind is called upon to do something it has never done before. And if he succeeds in this task, then his mind is forced to accept the "new normal." The bar has been raised. And so too must his level of performance. This is when *real growth* happens.

Intuitively, I think we all can distinguish "deliberate practice" from the moments when we're just "goofing around," "putting in the hours," or "watching the clock." We all understand that there is a big difference between someone who casually walks around the block once per day, and someone who sprints until his heart is about to burst. Both of these athletes may have put in the same number of hours, and yet only one of them is likely to significantly improve upon his running speed. As Ericsson notes:

With deliberate practice...the goal is not just to reach your potential but to build it, to make things possible that were not possible before. This requires challenging homeostasis—getting out of your comfort zone—and forcing your brain or your body to adapt... Excellence demands effort and planned, deliberate practice of increasing difficulty.

Not all of our hobbies and interests need be pursued with the same degree of dogged persistence. But, in our field of choice, extraordinary performance levels can only be obtained via a commitment to a continuous improvement process. This is why we study Kaizen. We aim to *thrive*, not just to survive. The methodology is not to be used as an excuse for complacency. Quite the opposite, as Kaizen's initial Western popularizer Masaaki Imai wrote:

Complacency is the arch-enemy of Kaizen.

We don't become Kaizen practitioners because we aim to devote a minimum amount of time to our labor. Instead, we practice Kaizen because we appreciate how very short our time on this planet is.

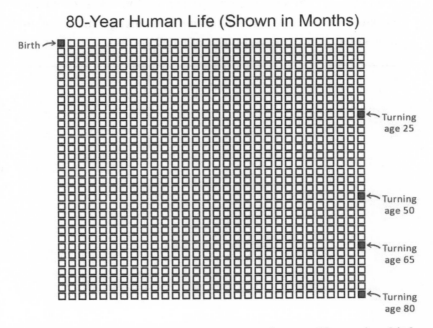

Figure 18 - In the Western world, the average human lifespan is a bit less than 80 years.

This image helps us to visualize the transient nature of our existence. Time is ticking away. Every minute counts. Many windows of opportunity lie before us. But, with each passing year, more and more windows will slide shut. Unfortunately, we don't have enough time to venture down every rabbit trail that streaks across our path. We have to choose our adventures carefully and plot our course with care, all while remaining mindful of the dissident tick of father time.

This is why developing your own personal productivity skillset is so crucial. Not only does Kaizen allow us to accomplish our goals more efficiently, but the methodology calls upon us to atomize each objective and focus the mind on its most essential constituents. As Greg McKeown (author of "Essentialism: The Disciplined Pursuit of Less") wrote:

Productivity is not about how to get *more* things done; it's about how to get the *right* things done. It doesn't mean just doing less for the sake of less... [It's] about making the wisest possible investment of your time and energy in order to operate at [your] highest point of contribution.

Ch. 8: Kaizen and Your Wealth

To develop a better understanding of Kaizen, we should take a moment to review the life and times of the man who was the originator of so many of its principles—the American engineer, statistician, and management consultant Dr. William Edwards Deming.

Born in Sioux City, Iowa in 1900, Deming obtained a bachelor's degree in electrical engineering in 1921 and a PhD in mathematics from Yale in 1928. He spent much of his early career studying statistical methods for industrial production, management, and quality control.

In 1950, Deming was invited to assist with post-World War II reconstruction efforts in Japan. Here, he delivered a series of lectures regarding the use of statistics for the improvement of production quality in manufacturing.

Figure 19 - W. Edwards Deming was invited to Japan to teach statistics for quality improvement by the Union of Japanese Scientists and Engineers.

In the years following World War II, Deming would make many trips to Japan—teaching hundreds of engineers, academics, and managers about his quality control techniques and management theories. His work was considered so essential to Japan's recovery that the Japanese Union of Scientists and Engineers named a medal after him. The "Deming Prize" is awarded to corporations or engineers who succeed in making a significant contribution to the field of quality control.

Figure 20 - Since 1951, the Deming Prize has been awarded to individuals and companies who have made significant advances in the field of manufacturing and quality control.

In 1985, the US Navy sought out civilian researchers to improve their operational effectiveness for statistical process control. Deming's well-referenced work was utilized, and the curriculum that came out of this undertaking came to be termed TQM (Total Quality Management). The TQM methodology remained popular throughout the 90s, and greatly influenced more recently introduced production methods and quality management systems like ISO 9000, Six Sigma, and Lean Manufacturing.

Deming's work remained relatively unknown to the American public until 1991 when he was the subject of Rafael Aguayo's book "Dr. Deming: The American Who Taught the Japanese about Quality." The book showcased Deming's management philosophy and remains popular with managers to this day.

Deming died in December of 1993, two months after his 93rd birthday. The work he produced in his lifetime could occupy hundreds of books. (The US Library of Congress has an entire audio and video collection featuring his curriculum.) But, in this chapter, I have attempted to surmise several of Deming's most pivotal ideas along with some ancillary contributions from other researchers in parallel fields. This information has been synergized into eight impactful principles—each designed to teach you how to effectively employ Kaizen in your own workplace endeavors.

Principle 1: Foster a continuous improvement mindset among yourself and your workforce

Throughout this book, we have repeatedly mentioned that each Kaizen exercise starts with one initial question:

What small step could I take today which may (in the long run) improve my situation?

This question was actually derived from the query that Edward Deming had each Toyota employee ask themselves at the start of every workday. His original question went like this:

What small step could I take today which may (in the long run) improve the process or product?

The ritual of asking the same question at the start of each workday helps the employee to focus his mind on the ultimate goal—the continuous improvement of the product, or the means by which the company builds the product. Of course, nobody expects each worker to arrive at a new epiphany every 24 hours. Instead, Deming's goal was merely to establish a proper frame of mind for the workforce. Asking employees to remain vigilant in their pursuit of productivity helps to deter complacency and readies the mind to spot a potentially big idea when one eventually surfaces.

Principle 2: Consider making a "little bet" on a potentially big idea

In utilizing the Kaizen methodology, managers hope to turn the workplace into an incubator for new ideas and serendipitous discoveries. When inspiration finally strikes and an idea shows promise, workers are granted the opportunity to implement and test the idea—if only for a day or two. This low-risk gambit is what management consultant Peter Sims would call a "little bet."

In his book, *"Little Bets: How Breakthrough Ideas Emerge from Small Discoveries"* Sims described how profitable outcomes are often the result of ventures that required a relatively small startup cost. E.g., an industrious individual spots a problem that needs solving, and then he makes a "little bet"—wagering his time and resources in the hopes of crafting a solution that people are willing to pay for.

Usually, such ploys don't amount to much. But sometimes the rewards are grand. This is why Google employees are allowed to dedicate 20% of their time to pet projects—ancillary pursuits that fall outside the scope of their day-to-day assignments. The vast majority of these projects never earn a single penny for Google. Most are a net drain on resources amounting to millions of dollars each year. However, it's only after you realize that Gmail, Google Maps, Google Adsense, and Google News all originated from such projects that the expense of their less successful peers is easier to rationalize.

Most moonshots fail to hit the moon. We can never know which modification to a workflow will result in increased efficiency, nor which one will hinder the process. But that's ok. Even if our idea doesn't pan out, we still haven't lost much. Because Kaizen bets are (by definition) "little bets."

Note that the Pareto Principle dictates that:

Roughly 80% of consequences will come from 20% of the causes.

In the business world, this means that:

- 80% of your sales come from 20% of your clients.
- 80% of your leads come from 20% of your ads.
- 80% of your revenue is generated by 20% of your products.

The potential solvency of any given business pursuit will forever remain mysterious to us. Hence, we are forced to instigate each campaign with the knowledge that failure is probable. This is part of the cost of doing business, but it is precisely *this* cost that Kaizen was developed to mitigate.

By breaking large projects down into smaller (less risky) steps ("little bets"), we curtail our losses when any given leap turns out to be less surefooted than we had originally hoped. If an undesirable outcome ensues, then we simply alter our course and try another path. This agile strategy is complemented by the incrementalist foundation that Kaizen is built upon. As Peter Sim wrote:

Finding ways to fail quickly, to invest less emotion and less time in any particular idea or prototype...is a consistent feature of the work methods of successful...innovators.

Principle 3: Foster pride of workmanship

In Chapter 3 we talked about the importance of engaging in activity that conjures the spirits of *Autonomy*, *Mastery*, and *Purpose*. If each emotion can be aroused during an employee's creative efforts, the synergy will result in an ethereal benefit—what Edward Deming liked to call "pride of workmanship."

In his book "Out of the Crisis," Deming explains:

...people that are measured by counting are deprived of *pride of workmanship*. The *"number of designs that an engineer turns out in a period of time"* would be an example of an index that provides no chance for pride of workmanship. He dare not take time to study and amend the design...to do so would decrease his output.

Deming was a statistician, but he was quick to note that an employee's worth is not so easily surmised by a single data point. Instead, fostering an environment in which work is completed with *pride* can be more valuable than any numerical measure of raw output. Landing a job that is capable of stirring such passions can be more important to the employee than any other executive amenity—particularly of the type that appears on a corporate brochure. As Deming wrote:

...*pride of workmanship* means more to the production worker than gymnasiums, tennis courts, and recreation areas... [Other than salary,] people require...their careers [to offer] ever-broadening opportunities—to add something to society, materially and otherwise.

How then does a boss make an employee understand that the cog he's producing is *important*, and that some degree of existential fulfillment is to be found in his profession?

Fans of Mike Judge's HBO series "Silicon Valley" might be familiar with a running joke on the show. Each time the characters interact with a new tech company, the CEO invariably insists that he is about to "change the world." The joke resonates with tech workers because *every* penniless tech startup in California claims to be on the verge of "changing the world"— no matter how trite their hot new mobile app actually is.

Still, their heart is in the right place. A good leader will perpetually remind his team of their raison d'etre. Often, the value of any given employee is obvious to the boss, but not to the employee himself. He might think of himself as a redundant gear in a meaningless clockwork. So a consistent effort must be made to show employees why and how their work is important—to the boss, the company, and to the customers.

The method by which such displays are rendered will vary from industry to industry. The gravitas of an employee's role might be exemplified by simply showing him exactly how his output affects his coworkers further down the supply chain or the production line. Or, his worth might also be revealed in a more artful manner. Steve Jobs famously had the signatures of the Apple development team branded to the back of every unit that came off the Mac assembly line. If you ever manage to get your hands on a 1984 Macintosh, you'll spot the signatures on the case's inside panel.

Figure 21 - Steve Jobs cast the signatures of the original Mac development team to the inside panel of the first Apple Mac.

Similar gestures can be found in many industries. It is good that such precious moments are ritualized. Recall the quote from David Deida that appears on the first page of this book:

Every moment of your life is either a test or a celebration.

Because so many hours of our lives are spent on the job, it is vital that we take a moment (every now and then) to celebrate and acknowledge the contributions of individual team members. One's profession is consistently cited as a driver of *life satisfaction*—reliably able to prod us to the top tiers of Maslow's *Hierarchy of Needs*. As a boss, manager, or team leader, anything you can do to hoist your employees up the ladder of self-actualization will result in greater job satisfaction for them, and more productive output for your company.

Given that the paths of one's work and home life are so often inextricably bound together, it is favorable that these courses run parallel—ideally leading to a mutually rewarding destination. As the Nobel Prize-winning economist Edmund Phelps wrote:

...Maslow coined [the term] "self-actualization" and John Rawls [coined] "self-realization" to refer to a person's emerging mastery and unfolding scope. [They] understood that most, if not all, of the attainable self-realization in modern societies can come only from *career*... If a challenging career is not the main hope for self-realization, what else could be?

Principle 4: "Drive out fear"

In an attempt to understand why so many communication problems plague corporations, Edward Deming would spend hours listening to audio tapes of conversations between factory workers and upper management. To his dismay, Deming noted that production problems often resulted from situations that line workers had identified long before catastrophe struck. But since they were too afraid to voice their concerns to upper management, the problems compounded—eventually leading to a dire situation. As Deming wrote:

No one can put in his best performance unless he feels secure. *"Se"* comes from the Latin, meaning without... *"Cure"* means fear or care. *"Secure"* means "without fear," not afraid to express ideas, not afraid to ask questions... Allow people to perform at their best by ensuring that they're not afraid to express [their unique] ideas or concerns.

For Deming, this freedom to "express their unique ideas or concerns" had a lot to do with providing employees with an opportunity to offer suggestions about how a process could be improved. Corporations naturally evolve hierarchies in which cross-department communication is stressed by cultural and social divides. Thus, managers must strive to ensure that the lines of communication remain open. Deming wrote:

Ensure that your leaders are approachable... Break down barriers between [departments]. People [working in] *research and design*...must learn about the problems encountered...[by the people working in] *production and assembly*.

Your team will understand that there isn't enough time in the day to implement every new proposal. But it should be made clear to them that there is no harm in making a suggestion. As the 16th-century Italian diplomat Niccolò Machiavelli wrote:

There is no other way to guard yourself against flattery than by making men understand that telling you the *truth* will not offend you.

Principle 5: The Seven Mudas

In Japanese, the word "muda" translates to "uselessness" or "wastefulness." The Japanese industrial engineer Taiichi Ohno codified his "Seven Mudas" while developing the Toyota Production System (TPS) during his thirty-year career with the company.

Figure 22 - Japanese industrial engineer Taiichi Ohno (1912-1990) was the father of the original Toyota Production System (TPS).

We'll discuss each of the Seven Mudas briefly here:

1. **Wasteful Motion**: The employee should have a workstation in which everything he needs to complete his job is available to him. The assembly of a product should not require him to take a circuitous route—retrieving tools or parts from far-off corners of the factory.

2. **Wasteful Transportation**: Moving a product costs money. If your product is bouncing between suppliers and distributors or accruing needless shipping costs, then there is a problem in your logistical infrastructure.

3. **Wasteful Waiting**: In any production process, products often spend most of their lives merely waiting to be worked on. Try to eliminate such periods of inactivity whenever possible.

4. **Wasteful Over-production**: Have you produced more products than you need or more than the market demands? Work to properly gauge future demand.

5. **Wasteful Over-processing**: Providing a customer with added value can be beneficial. But if the added features are not obvious to the customer, then the product has been over-engineered.

6. **Wasteful Inventory**: The longer your product sits unused or unpurchased, the more money it's costing you.

7. **Wasteful Defects**: A production line that produces too many duds is costly.

You don't need to own a factory to be mindful of the many types of similar inefficiencies that are quick to accumulate in any given work environment. Even the humblest small business is susceptible to the same sorts of resource-wasting hitches. In a typical office setting, such wastes often manifest in the form of *employee downtime*.

- Is your admin waiting for an email from your web developer?
- Is your web developer waiting for an email from your designer?
- Is your designer waiting for an email from your supplier?

When asked, most employees can readily cite multiple points of friction that hinder their daily productivity. Encouraging your team to remain cognizant of such workflow discrepancies (and to speak up when they know of a better way) will help to identify office waste and inefficiencies.

Principle 6: Identify your most crucial objectives

In Chapter 3, we discussed how the discovery of your Ikigai (your "true calling") can stir the forces of intrinsic motivation and help to combat crippling procrastination—of the sort that results in listlessness, inactivity, or the ardent refusal to do any work at all. But there are other types of procrastination. For entrepreneurs, their main problem is not that they fail to "show up at work" or "put in the hours." Instead, their preferred method of procrastination often takes on a more subtle role—colloquially termed "the busy idiot."

He's the guy who avoids doing the "real work" (i.e., the work that would actually benefit the company), instead electing to perform the easier (less mentally challenging) tasks first. When our mind is engaged in *some* sort of activity (any activity) then it is *much* easier to fool ourselves into believing that we're "doing work"—even if the task itself is wholly inconsequential. A *busy idiot* will bask in a milieu of frenzied action—if only to incite the transient psychological relief of knowing that he is (at least) "working on something." In the world of entrepreneurship, it is more common to meet a "busy idiot" than a "lazy person."

To avoid adopting this role, it helps to understand that your brain has a limited store of energy from which to draw upon. As each hour of the workday ticks by, *mental fatigue* will become an increasingly significant factor in every action you initiate. And, at the end of the day—when your brain has been entirely depleted of its energy—you won't be able to coax it into doing much more activity beyond eating and sleeping.

We can mitigate the deleterious effects of fatigue by rank-ordering our objectives—frontloading our most tedious tasks so that they are accomplished at the beginning of the workday when the mind is more tolerant of cognitively demanding challenges. As for our more inconsequential work functions, those should be pushed to the end of the day. These might include:

- Checking email
- Checking voicemail
- Tidying up the desk or workspace
- Organizing computer files
- Reading industry chatter
- Checking stock portfolios
- Categorizing expenditures

Of course, there is a time and a place for each of the above-listed tasks. But not all business pursuits improve your bottom line or "push the needle of success" with the same degree of force.

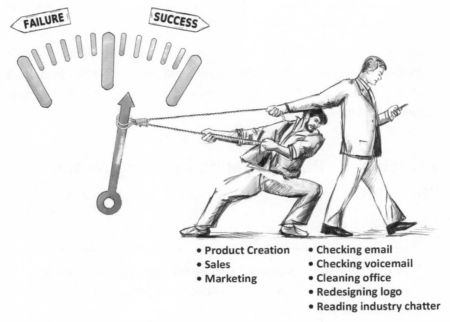

- Product Creation
- Sales
- Marketing

- Checking email
- Checking voicemail
- Cleaning office
- Redesigning logo
- Reading industry chatter

Figure 23 - The needle of success is typically advanced when resources are devoted to three things—product creation, sales, and marketing.

The most impactful actions tend to be in the domain of **product creation**, **sales**, and **marketing**. The actions you personally select to perform will be uniquely tailored to your industry. But it is probable that you already know which functions you *should* be executing each morning. I.e., you know which tasks would (if you were to actually get them done consistently) result in greater financial rewards.

In contrast to our previous list, a more impactful to-do list might look something like this:

- Reach out to five satisfied customers and ask them if they can recommend someone else who might also be interested in your product or service.

- Compose an email to your existing customer base and tell them about a new product or service that you'd like to offer them.
- Work with your developer to identify an area in which your product is currently lacking. Then devise a plan to improve the product's feature set.

Set yourself to the challenge of checking off your three most essential tasks each morning—*before* working on anything else. This will help to keep you on track and prevent you from losing sight of what a truly "productive day" looks like.

Principle 7: Focus means learning to say "no" a lot

Warren Buffett once said:

The difference between successful people and really successful people is that really successful people say "no" to almost everything.

Once you learn how to spot financial opportunities, then you'll notice that financial opportunities lurk behind every bend. They will forever be pining for your attention—eager to take a moment of your time and lure you away from your primary business objectives.

Some of these opportunities will sound very appealing. Some will be so good that you'll kick yourself for failing to act upon them—and maybe you should... But be warned; successful businesses are often highly specialized—good at providing one or two services or known for producing one or two successful products. It can be difficult to resist the temptation to keep adding ever more creations to your menu. But a good chef understands that "less is more."

When Steve Jobs regained control of Apple in 1998, he reportedly terminated 3,000 employees and reduced the number of Apple products from 350 to 10. In a conversation with Nike CEO Mark Parker, Jobs stated:

> **People think "focus" means saying "yes" to the thing you've got to focus on. But that's not what it means at all. It means saying "no" to the hundred other good ideas that there are. You have to pick carefully. I'm actually as proud of the things we haven't done as the things I have done. Innovation is saying "no" to 1,000 things.**

Principle 8: Be prepared for your chance meeting with fortune

The media loves to showcase rags-to-riches stories about industrialists who have managed to beat the odds, achieve extraordinary feats, and attain impossible financial victories. But such displays are usually just watercolor abstractions of the grim battles that entrepreneurs actually endure in pursuit of their goals. During such melodramas:

- You don't see the millions of mundane problems that the entrepreneur had to wrestle with each morning.
- You don't experience the waves of anxiety that wash across the body before a pivotal business decision is made.
- You don't live through the days when the company was hours away from bankruptcy or unable to make payroll.

In the real world, financial success seldom comes in the form of a graceful story arc. Unlike Archimedes, entrepreneurs rarely have a single *eureka moment*. Instead, success is achieved after years of mistakes, missteps, and blind stumblings across a highly competitive landscape.

Jim Collins (author of the 2001 bestseller *"Good to Great: Why Some Companies Make the Leap and Others Don't"*) spent his career studying the performance of exceptional companies. When questioning corporate managers about their breakout success, Collins was surprised to learn that few of them could pinpoint an inflection point at which it was clear that a meteoric rise to the top was inevitable. Three excerpts from his interviews are printed below:

Walgreens: **"There was no seminal meeting or epiphany moment, no one big bright light that came on like a lightbulb. It was sort of an evolution thing."**

Gillette: **"We didn't really make a big conscious decision or launch a big program to initiate a major change or transition. Individually and collectively we were coming to conclusions about what we could do to dramatically improve our performance."**

Philip Morris: **"It's impossible to think of one big thing that would exemplify a shift from good to great because our success was evolutionary as opposed to revolutionary, building success upon success. I don't know that there was any single event."**

In summarizing his findings, Collins wrote:

...it began to dawn on us [that] there was no *miracle moment*. Although it may have looked like a single-stroke breakthrough to those peering in from the outside, it was *anything but that* to [the] people experiencing transformation from within. Rather, it was a quiet, deliberate process of figuring out what needed to be done to create the best future results... And then simply taking those steps, one after the other, turn by turn of the flywheel. After pushing on that

flywheel in a consistent direction over an extended period of time, they'd inevitably hit a point of breakthrough.

The last sentence in this stanza is key; for it so nicely surmises the intent of the Kaizen philosophy—which emphasizes the consistent and disciplined application of daily ritual, routine, and habit. It is via a steadfast commitment to the pushing of the gears of industry that a profitable outcome will eventually spring forth.

Your career path will be dotted with serendipitous encounters and flashes of brilliant insight. But your ability to capitalize upon such incidents will be dependent upon your state of readiness—your willingness to show up at the office every day, put in the work, and keep an ear out for the sound of fortune's song. As the old adage states:

Luck is what happens when preparation meets opportunity.

This is true.

But we should take a moment to appreciate how elusive luck can be. Most of us will fail to recognize luck—even when it drops into our lap. Business success rarely comes in the form of a newly unearthed golden nugget. Instead, most fortunes are built upon a realization that is (at least initially) so mundane that the potential scale of its value is virtually imperceptible— even to the lucky man who stumbled upon it.

- Alexander Graham Bell's interest in telephone electronics was aimed at helping deaf people communicate.
- Bill Gates' first computer company was devoted to selling traffic monitoring switches to city planners.
- Google cofounder Larry Page unsuccessfully tried to sell off his search algorithm to Yahoo for a measly one million dollars.

Unfortunately, it is very difficult for the human mind to calculate more than one or two moves ahead on the grand chessboard of life.

- This is why we must remain vigilant at every stage of the game.
- This is why, with Kaizen, we don't pledge our commitment to the pursuit of a solitary lofty goal. Instead, we commit to the daily grind itself.

While we acknowledge that we can never know which turn of the flywheel will result in a bountiful reward, we also understand that fortune is more likely to come to the man who keeps pushing.

The Drunkard's Walk

In his New York Times bestselling book "The Drunkard's Walk: How Randomness Rules Our Lives" the American physicist Leonard Mlodinow discussed how the limitations of the human experience make it impossible for us to predict the future, and how our innate cognitive biases make it *very* easy for us to misinterpret the past.

Figure 24 - American theoretical physicist Leonard Mlodinow in 2012. (Photo by Martin Haburaj.)

While we'd all like to think that our bulletproof business plan will enable us to chart a decisive course to success, it is usually the case that such treks adopt a more circuitous route.

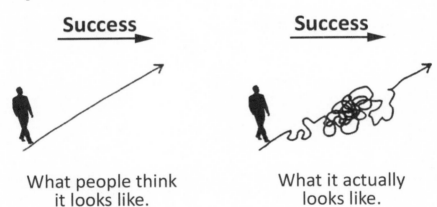

Figure 25 - Like a drunkard making his way home from a bar, the path to success typically only comes following a series of missteps and serendipitous encounters which cannot be anticipated.

Like a drunk hobbling to and fro as he makes his way home from the bar, the path of success is comparably serpentine. Life will present you with a never-ending succession of opportunities and setbacks. During this journey, you might drop out of school, switch careers, emigrate to a new country, get married, get divorced, have kids, quit your job, or go back to college.

- Which one of these actions was "the right move?" Which one was "the wrong move?"
- Which of these experiences turned out to be an asset? Which were liabilities?
- Which one was responsible for causing your venture to fail?
- Which one paved the road to your success?

Sometimes we can never know. Perhaps more often, we *think* we know, but our attempt to quantify the causal chain of past events is purely speculative.

This is why, with Kaizen, we attend to the pursuit of *daily progress* rather than devote much time to plotting a course to some *pie-in-the-sky* objective. As the Polish-American philosopher Alfred Korzybski would say, "The map is not the territory."

Figure 26 - Map of the allied invasion of Normandy, June 6, 1944. Field officers begin their mission with such maps, but they must improvise and adapt to ever-changing battle conditions.

Any strategy that we would bother to formulate will inevitably be sidelined by the chaotic exigencies of the battlefield. Our best-laid plans quickly morph into mere approximations of our grand designs. As Henry Mintzberg (co-author of the seminal paper "Of Strategies, Deliberate and Emergent") wrote:

Strategy emerges over time as intentions collide with (and accommodate) a changing reality.

Good entrepreneurs must forever strive to keep their business pursuits agile enough to recognize a "better path" when one reveals itself. Serendipitous encounters may lead the company in a different direction. And often, the product that results from this course correction will achieve a utility that far surpasses the initial goal of its originators.

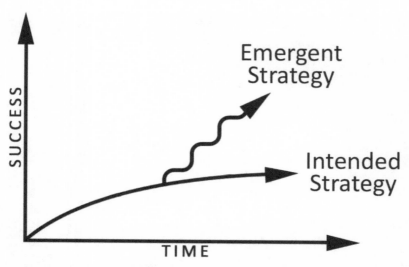

Figure 27 - Emergent strategies tend to naturally evolve out of intended strategies, and often lead to more fortunate outcomes.

Such is the evolutionary reality of business innovation. We might spend long hours on market research and analysis—attempting to account for every possible contingency. But, ultimately, none of us really know which business idea will be profitable until somebody "takes a shot" and tries to implement it.

This is why, with Kaizen, we understand that there is no "high ground" that demarks the end of our march. Our primary objective is the pursuit of continuous improvement itself. No matter our present circumstances, we commit to press on. We take shot, after shot, after shot, after shot. And if we take enough shots, we know that one of them is bound to result in a winning goal.

As Leonard Mlodinow concluded:

What I've learned, above all, is to keep marching forward... [Though] chance does play a role, one important factor in success is under our control: the number of "at bats," the number of chances taken, the number of opportunities

seized. For even a coin weighted toward failure will sometimes land on success.

Ch. 9: Kaizen and Your Health

Reality TV fans will likely recall the hit weight-loss show *The Biggest Loser*. The original incarnation of the show debuted on NBC in the fall of 2004 and ran for 17 seasons before moving to the USA Network in 2020. Every week, twelve obese contestants would compete against each other—racing to lose the highest percentage of bodyweight relative to their initial starting weight. At the show's dramatic conclusion, before-and-after images reveal the amazing body transformations that each contestant had achieved. Then, a prize is awarded to the winner. And everyone goes home.

But what happens after that?

Researchers at the US National Institute of Health managed to convince the Season 8 contestants to enroll in a longitudinal weight loss study. The results surprised even the seasoned diet scientists. The majority of *Biggest Loser* contestants regained much of their lost body weight in the months following the show's finale. As New York Times writer Gina Kolata reported:

> **What shocked the researchers was what happened next: As the years went by and the numbers on the scale climbed, the contestants' metabolisms did not recover... It was as if their bodies were intensifying their effort to pull the contestants back to their original weight.**

The big secret about *The Biggest Loser* is that almost every contestant on the show eventually becomes "big" again. That is to say, almost all the contestants are now fat.

These dismaying results exemplify the inadequacies of conventional goal setting. Weight loss goals in particular are notoriously fallible. The complete process often looks something like this:

- First, the overweight person pledges to lose several pounds.
- They then select a target date that often corresponds with an upcoming social gathering, like a wedding or a class reunion.
- When the big day finally arrives, our subject has either failed to achieve her goal, or she gladly reveals her new bodyweight for all to admire.
- Then, once the grand gala is over, so too is the primary motivator for our subject's weight loss routine. As the weeks progress, the pounds pile back on, and the needle on her scale returns to its former position.

The flaws in this goal-setting schema are easy to spot. An objective of this sort (e.g., maintaining a certain bodyweight) will require a lifetime of daily commitments to attain. When the motivation to complete such a task is punctuated by a crescendo of social pressure (of the sort experienced by a bride preparing for her wedding day or by a contestant on *The Biggest Loser*), then positive outcomes are often transient. Once the party is over and the external drivers have been removed, failure soon follows.

In the previous chapter, we mentioned Dr. Richard Wiseman's 2007 study on New Year's Resolutions. Here, it was revealed that 88% of resolutions fail soon after the holiday ends. But we neglected to mention one curious finding from the study. When participants committed to a "weekly goal" instead of a single long-term goal, then their chance of success went up by 22%. The subjects were more likely to stick with their New Year's Resolution when the activity was to be completed in a small and measurable timeframe. For example, a goal to "lose five pounds each month" had a higher chance of success than a goal to simply "lose 20 pounds this year."

It is exactly this sort of incrementalist strategy that powers the Kaizen methodology. If you want to adopt a fit lifestyle and maintain a healthy body weight for life, then periodically starving yourself to achieve a solitary victory is *not* recommended. Instead, achieving such a goal requires a commitment to daily habits. Of course, in Kaizen, that's what we're all about.

In this chapter, we'll discuss several tips to help you develop your own Kaizen-inspired nutrition and fitness regimen.

Part 1: Weight loss and Nutrition with Kaizen

Tip #1: Make a list of all the unhealthy foods you consume each day

Achieving good nutrition hinges upon your willingness to fill your stomach with "good foods" while simultaneously avoiding the "bad foods." Innumerable lists of healthy and unhealthy foods can be found online—many of them quite contradictory to each other. But, it is likely the case that you already have a pretty good idea about which foods you should *not* be eating.

As we reach for the box of microwave pizza in the freezer section of our local supermarket, most of us know that we're not making the best dietary decision. In America, the consumption of ultra-processed food is particularly troubling. These include:

1. potato chips
2. candy
3. cakes
4. cookies
5. donuts

6. ice cream
7. french fries
8. hot dogs
9. instant noodles
10. sugary soft drinks

It's universally agreed upon that extracting these ten items from our diet would result in substantial health benefits for the populace. This is not to say that we should never enjoy a snack. But our goal should be to curtail the consumption of ultra-processed food as much as possible.

So how do we pursue this objective?

As the management guru Peter Drucker liked to say:

What gets measured gets managed.

So start by maintaining a log of each ultra-processed morsel that you consume during the week. Don't make the task complicated. (You don't need an app for this.) Instead, try a simpler approach:

1. Keep a piece of paper with you and list each unhealthy food item as you encounter it throughout the day. You can use the above-listed ten food groups if you're unsure about which items you should be tracking.
2. Then, during the week, put a checkmark next to the food group each time you consume a portion of it.
3. When Sunday comes, count the number of checkmarks that you have accumulated on your page.
4. When a new week begins, pull out a new piece of paper and repeat this process.

Our goal, of course, is to reduce the number of checkmarks that appear on the page each week. Each new document is a new opportunity to reduce the total tally—thus mitigating the amount of processed food we consume. Of course, you can use the same method to track the number of *healthy foods* you consume each week too. For example, every time you eat a serving of broccoli put a checkmark in the "vegetables" category.

You may never be able to end the week with a perfect record—completely free of unhealthy checkmarks. And nor would you really want to. Sampling rich food is one of life's many joys. But, your goal should be to monitor and minimize your daily consumption of junk food items—until they become an occasional snack, and not a principal part of your diet.

Tip #2: Frontload your calories

There's a well-known fitness maxim (popularized by the mid-20th century nutritionist Adelle Davis) which states:

Eat breakfast like a king, lunch like a prince, and dinner like a pauper.

Unfortunately, it is typical for time-strapped urbanites to rush through morning breakfast, instead electing to devour junk food on the way to work or between meetings. Lunch might be consumed in a similarly frenzied manner. Some of us try to compensate for this caloric deficit with a large dinner—often consisting of burgers or burritos consumed in front of the TV.

Such undesirable eating rituals may be contributing to the US obesity epidemic. Several studies indicate that the "hour of the day" at which we consume our meals is a factor in weight gain. Merely frontloading calories may help to keep the pounds off.

In a 2013 research project led by Daniela Jakubowicz of Tel Aviv University, 93 obese or overweight women were placed into two groups and put on the same low-calorie diet. Only their breakfast and dinner portion sizes varied.

- The "Big Dinner" group was given a 200-calorie breakfast and a 700-calorie dinner.

- The "Big Breakfast" group was given a 700-calorie breakfast and a 200-calorie dinner.

At the end of the twelve-week study, both groups had lost weight, but the "Big Breakfast" group had lost 11 more pounds than the "Big Dinner" group.

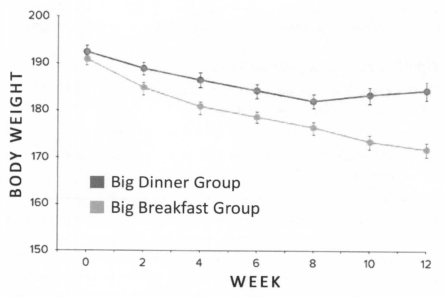

Figure 28 - Upon completion of a twelve-week weight loss program, subjects who ate a big breakfast but a small dinner, lost 11 more pounds than the subjects who ate a smaller breakfast but a large dinner. (Source: Daniela Jakubowicz, Maayan Barnea, Julio Wainstein, Oren Froy (2013) High Caloric Intake at Breakfast vs. Dinner Differentially Influences Weight Loss of Overweight and Obese Women, doi:10.1002/oby.20460)

More recently, a 2014 study by *The American College of Nutrition* divided 42 subjects into two groups and fed them a similarly skewed menu: one group consumed 45% of their calories at dinner while the other ate 35% at dinner. Again, the "small dinner group" lost more weight, prompting the researchers to conclude:

One clear communication from physicians could be, "If you want to lose weight, eat more in the morning than in the evening."

Of course, we should note that merely skipping dinner is not necessarily indicative of a healthy lifestyle. Individuals in a high-stress environment might be consuming snack food all day and then skipping dinner due to fatigue. Obviously, this sort of lifestyle is not ideal. No matter what time you eat, you should still try to fill your stomach with healthy meals. But frontloading calories seems to aid in metabolic processing and should help to mitigate weight gain.

Tip #3: Reduce the amount of time you spend sitting

Regardless of the amount of time you spend in the gym, physical fitness should be a persistent part of your daily lifestyle. Unfortunately, urbanites often commute to work by car, scale parking garage levels in an escalator, and then ascend to an office floor via elevator. This effortless trek is followed by eight hours of sitting in a desk chair.

The demands of the modern world do not call upon us to use our muscles very often. But, by making small lifestyle alterations, we can increase the number of physical activities that we perform each day. Here are a few suggestions:

- **Stand up more during the workday**. To counteract the deleterious health effects of sitting at a desk all day, try conducting your work functions in a more elevated state. You might consider standing during some workday activities such as placing phone calls, waiting for printers to print, checking email, conducting meetings, or eating lunch. If you're serious about keeping things vertical, consider taking the plunge and trading your office desk in for a "stand-up desk."

- **Park your car farther from your destination**. If you commute to work each day, then consider parking your car as far from your building's front entrance as possible—so you can burn a few calories and stretch your legs during the morning approach. Aside from the office parking lot, consider utilizing this trick at other destinations too—like during your weekly visit to the grocery store or mall. Ideally, you'll be able to park your car such that you get a bit of exercise done at each waypoint. Of course, if the weather permits and the location is proximate, you can always walk or bike to your destination.

- **Avoid elevators and take the stairs**. Every building with an elevator also has stairs. So consider using the latter over the former. If your office or apartment is too high to get to via stairs alone, then just use the stairs for a portion of the journey, and consider incrementally adding additional flights each week.

- **Pick a sport or hobby that requires physical activity**. Intense physical exertion is a lot more fun when it comes in the form of competition. If interval training and body-building are not your thing, there are other ways to get a healthy workout. Do you play tennis or soccer? Have you considered joining a hiking group, a dance class, or taking up gardening? If you can foster positive emotions when performing a particular outdoor activity, then the act of exertion will not be so grueling. You may even come to look forward to it.

Tip #4: Use psychology to curtail hunger

Like so much of Asian philosophy, many Kaizen principles were developed to complement the peculiarities of human psychology. We are wise to remain mindful of the innumerable networks that are forever activating in the depths of our brains. The feeling of satiation is incited by complex circuitry which may be triggered by multiple forms of external stimuli. Via introspection, you should be able to take note of the stimuli that affects you the most. If walking by the cookie jar causes you to reach for a 200-calorie chocolate chip cookie, then perhaps you shouldn't have a cookie jar in your house? This leads to our first tip:

- **Do not store unhealthy snacks in your proximity**. One of the easiest ways to prevent yourself from snacking on high-calorie junk food is to simply make it inaccessible—i.e., don't store any bags of chips, candies, or cookies in your home. This is not to say that you can never snack on these items. But buy them in single-serving portions and consume them immediately after purchase. By invoking this rule, we create a buffer between your appetite and the unhealthy food of your desire. The more footsteps that exist between you and the candy, the less likely you'll be to eat it. Brian Wansink (author of *Mindless Eating: Why We Eat More Than We Think*) is famous for putting candy dishes near the desks of office workers and then recording them as they toss hundreds of empty calories into their mouths throughout the workday. It's difficult for your lower brain to ignore such a tasty stimuli— especially when it is so proximate to your hand. So don't put your brain through that. Instead, adhere to the old proverb: "out of sight, out of mind."
- **Drink more water**. The brain has trouble differentiating between a stomach full of food and a stomach full of water. Drinking a full glass of water (about 350 milliliters) before each meal may help to incite satiety.
- **Give your brain a minute to catch up with your stomach**. Be mindful of the lag that exists between the swallowing of each bite of food and the onset of satiation. It's commonly reported that it takes twenty minutes to experience the feeling of fullness. But the time will vary depending on many factors, including your personal physiology and the accessibility and novelty of the food on the table before you. If you've just devoured a slice of cake, and you're currently eyeing a second slice, then try removing it from your field of view and make a deal with yourself—give yourself

permission to eat the second slice if you're still hungry in twenty minutes. You might find that its appeal has faded by the time the twenty minutes is up.

- **Ritualize the process of saving restaurant food for later**. Retail sales for US restaurants and bars overtook grocery store sales in January of 2015. Meaning that Americans now spend more money *eating out* than they do *eating in*. When we dine at a restaurant or fast-food eatery, it is natural to want to consume every food item on the plate. But, given the absurdity of contemporary American portion sizes, there is usually too much to eat. In nearly every food category, US portion sizes have increased—often served in amounts that are 3 to 8 times larger than a standard FDA serving. Conventional dieting advice would propose that we simply eat less food—regardless of the amount that is served before us. But it is difficult to rationalize the expense of walking away from a half-eaten restaurant meal that has already been paid for. To account for these conflicting emotions, get in the habit of stowing a portion of your meal each time you eat out. Since restaurant doggie bags are typically not airtight, consider carrying a small Tupperware container with you during your lunch break. And order your meal with the intent of taking some portion of it home with you. Our aim is to make a habit out of reducing the restaurant's default portion size—at least whenever logistically possible and when dining decorum permits.

Tip #5: Measure your progress ritualistically

As discussed in Chapter 5, the 6th Principle of Kaizen calls upon us to "measure results ritualistically." Of course, this principle is all the more crucial when it comes to the monitoring of personal weight loss goals. A typical dieter's log often consists of weekly weigh-ins or daily calorie counts. But many other tracking methods exist. You could measure your:

- Body Mass Index (BMI)
- Waist Circumference

- Estimated Body Fat (using calipers, bioelectrical impedance / "smart scales," or hydrostatic weighing)
- Or, you might even try photographing your body once a month.

Be aware that estimating body fat and gauging dietary progress are notoriously error-prone processes. All of these methods are open to criticism and subject to significant miscalculations. But for a conventional weight loss routine, that's ok. Our goal here is not to earn a PhD in diet science. Instead, our goal is to create a daily ritual in which your mind is reminded of your commitment to weight loss each time you step up to the scale, pull out the calipers, or jot down the number of calories in that bucket of chicken you're about to eat.

Even if the errors in your measurements are substantial, the values will still be useful so long as they are (at least) *directionally* correct. As the months go by, seeing a (perhaps jittery but ever-declining) line on your progress chart will motivate you to stick to your regimen. Learning to manage your nutritional lifestyle entails first learning how to measure the undesirable dietary inputs that have brought it about. Recall our Peter Drucker quote again:

What gets measured gets managed.

Part 2: Physical fitness with Kaizen

While weight loss goals are obtained via the regulation of bodily inputs (i.e., food), fitness and strength training goals are achieved when the body's muscles encounter resistance. Conditioning the body requires a long-term commitment to daily exercise—one that very few of us have the willpower to maintain for long.

For those who do manage to muster the motivation to hit the gym, their initial inspiration often comes after viewing adverts featuring toned models, athletes, or muscular Marvel superheroes. A weight-challenged individual might see Jason Momoa's impressive physique in the film *Aquaman*, and then race down to his local health club to demand a lifetime membership. But shortly after stepping onto the rubberized flooring, the euphoria of his spontaneous decision begins to dissipate. He may soon realize that repetitively hoisting black iron is boring, difficult, and exhausting. As this fatigue devolves into apathy, he may lose the desire to drive to the gym every evening after work. Eventually, the only reminder of his initial commitment will be an unused gym membership card—which now sits abandoned in the recesses of his wallet.

People are good at recognizing the value of a finished product. But lousy at discerning the number of steps required for its construction. The artful appeal of a celebrity's chiseled chest belies the grueling hours of labor that went into creating it. Several months before principal photography, Jason Momoa's workout regimen demanded five days a week of weight training and multiple cardio activities including hill sprints and rock climbing. This level of exertion resulted in an amazing body that lasted about as long as it was needed—from the first day of filming to the final photography session for the movie poster and marketing media. When the show is over, our superheroes go home. The handlers that ushered them through the gym doors each morning are off to work on another film. Consequently, the pounds pile on, and their daily reps decrease. As Momoa himself stated:

I don't like going [to the] gym [and] I don't touch a weight unless they're paying me to do it...

What are your personal fitness goals?

While there are some men out there who manage to maintain a superhero physique for life, most of us are better off pursuing more realistic goals. In the proceeding section, we'll be discussing how you can construct a personal fitness regimen utilizing the Kaizen methodology. But be warned:

- Kaizen is not a good approach to strength training if you're about to star in a Hollywood superhero film.
- Kaizen techniques won't be applicable if you're entering a bodybuilding, boxing, or MMA competition next month.
- Kaizen will not get you to the Olympics.

Instead, the Kaizen approach is for the rest of us; for those who seek to remain fit in perpetuity. And for those who are willing to commit to pursuing a lifetime of daily strength-training goals. The following four tips describe how to apply Kaizen to these objectives.

Tip #1: Do *not* sign up for a gym membership

At some point in your life, you probably had access to a gym or paid for a gym membership. And, chances are, you probably didn't go very often.

How do I know that?

In January of 2020, the consumer comparison website Finder.com surveyed 2,400 US adults about their gym membership usage. In summarizing their data, Finder reported that a whopping 49% of members admitted to only utilizing the gym "once a week or never." Even more disheartening, Finder estimated that Americans waste roughly $1.8 billion each year on gym memberships that are never used at all.

- So why are so many Americans paying for a service that they rarely use?
- What's preventing these people from hitting the gym each evening after work?
- Why do so many of us fail to accomplish our strength-training goals?

Remember, when we take a Kaizen approach to problem-solving, we first step back and observe the current inefficiencies of the process. Consider the many familiar points of friction that a gym membership entails:

- First, gyms are rarely within walking distance of the member's home. This means that he must get into his car and drive to the facility. Arriving at the location means parking the car, grabbing a gym bag, and marching to the front entrance. All of these steps require time. Often, the journey to the gym can take up more time than the workout itself.

- Once our member steps foot through the gym's front entrance, the problems continue. He might have to queue up for a complicated check-in process and display his credentials to the insufferable staff. Next comes the locker room, where our member must stow his keys, cellphone, and gym bag. Then he must change into his workout attire.

- When he finally arrives at the gym floor, our member must brave the critical eyes of his fellow gym rats. While it is likely that nobody even knows he's there, the anxious mind tends to assume that everyone is evaluating everyone else's physique (or lack thereof).

- Strolling over to the weight machine, our member must wipe away the sweat residue of the previous user, and then begin his maneuvers—hoping that the other (supposedly more experienced) members won't be critiquing his novice form and technique.

- Finally, when his workout is complete, it's time for our member to exit the facility. He must perform all of the above steps in reverse; grabbing his gear, changing his clothes, getting back into his car, and making the long journey home.

In examining the preceding steps, it's clear that our member must devote a colossal amount of time and effort to merely moving his body to the gym. This inefficiency is a perfect example of the first of the "Seven Mudas" discussed in the previous chapter. "Wasteful motion" occurs when the laborer is required to take a circuitous route to generate a product. E.g., if you spend two hours of your life trying to get a 20-minute workout in, then your efforts are *wasteful*.

Additionally, the typical gym membership schema is laden with hindrances that are prone to incite undesirable mental triggers. If the task of merely "getting to the gym" is physically and psychologically exhausting, then your lower mind will try to prevent you from pursuing this course of action by summoning a million excuses:

- There's too much traffic on the road.
- There's not enough gas in the car.
- It's too hot today.
- It's too cold today.
- It's gonna rain.
- It's snowing.
- It's Sunday.
- Your favorite show is on TV.
- Your friend is flying in for a visit.
- You have to wake up early for work tomorrow.
- You don't want to sweat before a date.
- You don't want to sweat before bed.
- You don't like to sweat anyway.

It's difficult for the brain to muster the willpower necessary to handle all of life's daily tragedies, and then have enough discipline left over to drive to a smelly building and lift iron plates for an hour. This is why most of us never use our gym membership cards. And why almost all of us eventually cancel.

Quite disheartening…

But there exists an alternate solution to our dilemma.

Tip #2: Build your own "home gym"

The many systemic limitations inherent in a conventional gym membership model make "going to the gym" an inefficient and tedious process. But you can avoid these drawbacks by designing your own "home gym."

Don't worry; we're not talking about hiring a contractor to add an additional room to your house. Instead, your "home gym" might simply consist of a few dumbbells nestled in the corner of your apartment. By carving out a domain dedicated to the chore of exercise, we hope to mitigate some of the many impediments that prevent us from completing our evening workout.

Critics of the "home gym" paradigm will be quick to note that merely constructing a home gym does not guarantee its use. Residential garages often function as graveyards for petrified exercise equipment—metal contraptions purchased long ago and at great expense, but only used one time.

So why does this happen?

Why do so many home workout machines sit unused? What prevented you from installing that $400 exercise machine that you bought at Walmart ten years ago?

Just as the conventional gym membership model has many potential pitfalls, so to does the home gym approach. In this section, we'll discuss how our efforts to exercise at home are often thwarted by two common gym design mistakes:

1. An improperly selected gym environment
2. Improperly selected gym equipment

Mistake #1: An improperly selected gym environment

When constructing a home gym, people often make the mistake of placing their newly purchased gym equipment in the least desirable room in the

158

house—such as a garage, a storage shed, a workroom, a porch, or a backyard patio. But positioning gym equipment in the periphery of your home often causes you to push your workout commitments to the periphery of your mind. Does your garage look anything like the following photo?

Figure 29 - A collapsible exercise bike sits unused in this crowded and dirty garage.

Here, a lonely exercise bike sits collecting dust near the family car. It lies wedged between a bag of golf clubs and a box of Christmas ornaments. This image is the quintessential representation of a bad home gym design. To understand why this is the case, consider the many questions that most people fail to consider when constructing their home workout area.

- Does the location get too cold in winter? Or too hot in summer?
- Does the workout area have a bad smell or poor airflow?
- Does it get too noisy when the washing machine is running?
- Is it too humid when the dryer is running?
- Does the workout area lack any form of entertainment like a TV, radio, or media station?
- Is the area too small? Does your bench press bar scrape along the wall when you're doing reps?

- Can you work out when the car is parked in the garage? Or only when it's in the driveway?

Your lower mind will use each one of these little annoyances as an excuse to *not* work out. If you have to back out the family car each time you use your Soloflex Home Workout Station, then you are *not* going to use your Soloflex Home Workout Station.

The path to your home gym must be free of complexifiers, hindrances, and obstacles of every sort. Because:

As the number of obstacles that stand between you and your workout machine *increases*, the chance that you will actually use the workout machine *decreases*.

This is why your home gym equipment should be proximate to the rooms in your house where "life happens"—typically the kitchen, the bedroom, or the home office. In glancing at the exercise bike in the proceeding image, you should be able to discern how its location facilitates its use—especially when contrasted to the bike in our previous garage photo.

Figure 30 - In this stylish home office, a Peloton Exercise Bike (with attached video display) is proximate to the owner's workstation.

Your workout area should be *part of your life*—not separate from it. Your home gym equipment should be located in the room you feel most comfortable in—preferably a well-trekked and temperature-controlled area that you frequently utilize, even when you're not working out.

By integrating the workout task with your other daily life functions, we aim to reduce the size of the mental hurdles that span between you and the execution of your exercise routine. When the chore of daily fitness becomes a habit, starting your home workout shouldn't require any more willpower than starting your home microwave.

Mistake #2: Improperly selected gym equipment

Once you've managed to find a suitable workout location, it's time to select your home gym equipment. If you stroll down the fitness aisle of your favorite big box store, you'll see plenty of "As Seen on TV" ab crunch trainers and workout machines of questionable build quality. You'll pretty much want to avoid all of these devices—especially the ones that claim to be "foldable" or "portable." To understand why, try to perceive the workout task from the perspective of your lower mind. Recall the adage discussed earlier in this book:

Your brain exists to help you survive, not to thrive.

Your lizard brain doesn't understand why you're asking it to lift metal bars or run in a circle. No wild animal is chasing you. No band of marauders is hunting you down. So why are you running?

When your lower mind is at rest, it would prefer to stay at rest. It evolved during a time when food was scarce. So expending precious calories on your stupid new fitness hobby is not a project that it perceives as being worth the risk. Consequently, it will use any potential annoyance to dissuade you from initiating the workout task. This is why, in the previous section, we took care to identify the many potential pain points that can deplete one's willpower in a conventional gym membership model. Of course, when it comes to constructing our home gym, we must be mindful of similar impediments.

Avoid purchasing any piece of gym equipment that can't be used until it is extended, repositioned, unscrewed, stowed away, or unfolded. We've listed four examples of such machines in the proceeding image.

Gym equipment that you should <u>NOT</u> buy.

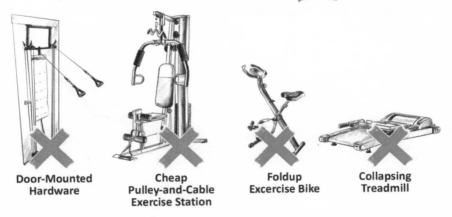

Door-Mounted Hardware

Cheap Pulley-and-Cable Exercise Station

Foldup Excercise Bike

Collapsing Treadmill

Figure 31 - Home gym equipment is often poorly constructed and requires a troublesome setup process that makes it undesirable for daily use.

Most of us have had an experience with at least one of these devices.

- Door-mounted workout contraptions (especially elastic bands) are unsightly, and the setup process often renders the door itself inoperable.
- Complex pulley-and-cable machines ("home gym workstations") are notoriously difficult to set up and are comprised of a Rube Goldberg-like conglomeration of wires and wheels that are infamously error-prone.
- Fold-up exercise bikes usually remain folded up in the closet.
- And collapsing treadmills usually remain collapsed under the bed.

Additionally, low-build-quality machines tend to creek or bend during use. Cheap treadmills wobble, bicycle pedals don't spin, cables don't flow, and pulleys don't turn. If your equipment doesn't enable each maneuver to be executed in a solid and fluid progression, then your brain will dissuade you from executing the maneuver.

So what sort of exercise equipment should you buy then?

If this is your first exposure to the world of fitness or strength training, it's best to keep things simple. Resist the temptation to buy complicated workout machines. You can get a full-body workout with a single set of dumbbells and an adjustable bench.

Figure 32 - A dumbbell rack and bench are all you need to get a full-body workout.

Innumerable dumbbell workouts can be found online. Many are geared toward people with minimal gym equipment and minimal time at their disposal. If you'd like a suggestion, check out Jeff Cavaliere of Athlean-X Fitness. He sells training programs via his website, but you can find plenty of free dumbbell-only workouts on his YouTube channel—which (at time of publication) has amassed an incredible 11 million subscribers.

But regardless of the type of workout you choose, don't let information overload prevent you from taking immediate action. In designing your home gym, your initial objective should be focused on *habit-building,* not *strength-training.* You can start by purchasing a single pair of dumbbells and pumping out a single set of curls once a day—Monday through Friday. The entire routine should take less than a minute to complete.

Does that sound doable?

This achievement is modest to the point of being laughably small.

It's intended to be.

Remember, in Kaizen, our initial goal is to do one "laughably small" task first. In doing so, our aim is not to build muscle but to build psychological momentum and prompt your new fitness habit to take hold in your brain. We want your lower mind to get used to the idea that it will be pumping iron every evening after work. Doing a single set of dumbbell curls sounds diminutive and pointless. But if you can actually perform this task each day for a week, then your workout regimen will be far superior to that of the majority of the populace—who don't work out at all.

Sadly, most people will not succeed in maintaining a daily commitment of even this minuscule caliber. But if you can keep it up for a while, then you're one of the enlightened few. And it will be time to consider expanding your workout regimen—gradually moving on to progressively heavier weights and higher rep counts. We'll be talking about this incrementalist approach to fitness in the next section.

For now, I hope this chapter has convinced you of the importance of devising *some* sort of daily home fitness regimen. The Kaizen approach to strength training will not turn you into a competitive bodybuilder overnight. Instead, we just want to get you to actually enter your home gym each evening and lift some weight. Recall that the majority of paying gym membership holders do not even do that much.

Tip #3: Track your daily fitness activity

Throughout this book, we have repeatedly stressed the importance of tracking your results in every endeavor you pursue. Of course, when it comes to your strength-training goals, the same rule applies. Once you've decided to execute a workout regimen, it's vital that you log your progress in some fashion. Typical metrics include:

- The amount of weight on the bar (aka poundage)
- The number of reps
- The number of sets
- The tonnage (weight x reps)
- The number of push-ups

- The number of sit-ups
- The number of miles pedaled
- The number of miles walked
- The number of miles jogged
- Etc.

Countless apps and charts can be downloaded online for tracking and monitoring your fitness progress. Personally, I find mobile apps to be too tedious for data entry in the gym. I've been tracking my weight, caloric intake, and workout metrics in a single Microsoft Excel spreadsheet for a decade. But the medium you use to log these stats is not important. What's important is that you get in the habit of logging *something*.

The utility of recording daily fitness metrics should be obvious to everyone. Yet, it is rare to meet a person who can look back into their logs and tell you exactly how much weight they were benching on the second Tuesday of December in 2017. (On that day I had 190 pounds on the bar.)

Remember, in Kaizen we love data. But we don't necessarily keep track of our metrics because we expect our logs to reveal something insightful or revolutionary about our workout technique. Instead, we track our daily fitness progress for the same reason that Jerry Seinfeld tracked his daily joke-writing progress. Because ritualizing and gamifying the process helps us to *stick to the process*.

Your fitness log is your trophy case—a visual reminder of your past workout successes. Every dumbbell rep is a victory. Every completed routine is a prize. By religiously logging your stats, you should be able to see a steady incremental increase in your levels of daily physical exertion. In observing a record of how far you have come, your mind will be better able to summon the motivation needed to push yourself ever farther.

Tip #4: Gradually increase your workout intensity

Given that the Kaizen approach to strength training is a multi-decade endeavor, our primary gym objective is to gradually build muscle while avoiding injury. When we're lifting, we focus on form, not tonnage. We attune our posture and perform graceful maneuvers that move the weight in a controlled fashion. Most importantly, we avoid the natural tendency to add more weight to the bar when our muscles are not yet ready.

Bodybuilders have big egos. And it's common for them to size each other up based on their rep count or plate loadout. This causes many newbies to sacrifice form for heavier plates. Pushing your muscles to their absolute (rip and tear) brink may have a place in competitive sports. But our aim is merely to stress the body enough to add muscle and get a workout.

The incrementalist strategy that Kaizen advocates is not unlike many other strength-training methodologies—which call upon the practitioner to gradually increase the intensity and duration of a workout session until the fitness goal is achieved. But the nuance lies in understanding the types of objectives that this long-view approach to fitness will not apply to. In Kaizen:

- We are not "crash dieters" or fitness models.
- We don't race to lose ten pounds for a wedding party.
- We don't diet just to fit into a new pair of jeans.
- We don't starve ourselves to get "beach body ready" for summer.
- And we're not going to be on the cover of *Men's Health Magazine* next week.

Additionally, we are not "extreme athletes."

- We don't plan on winning any weightlifting competitions.
- We're not going to be in an MMA championship event.
- We don't play in the NFL.
- And we're not going to compete in the Olympics.

Achieving such goals require commitments that are not practical for the majority of the population. The few brave souls who do engage in such pursuits usually only do so for very brief periods of their lives. Keeping their body in "fighting shape" requires a lifestyle that would not be feasible for most of us.

The 23-time Olympic gold medal winner Michael Phelps has an amazing physique. But at what cost? In his autobiography "No Limits," Phelps reported that during training he'd spend five hours in a pool each morning and consume ten thousand calories a day. His meals consisted of (as he put it) "pretty much anything I wanted."

Such physical feats should be acknowledged for their entertainment value. But they ought not be pursued as a life strategy. You have better things to do with your time than swim in a circle for five hours. This is why you must learn to be comfortable with a slow and gradual pursuit of your fitness goals. This strategy lies in contrast to the oft-advertised "crash diets" or "muscle man workouts" that promise to help you "get shredded in 30 days or less." The main fault in such extreme regimens is not that they "don't work." (Almost every fitness plan works to some degree.) Instead, the miscalculation comes when you realize that, after the 30 days are up, you still have a lot of days left in your life.

There's an old proverb (commonly misattributed to Confucius) that states:

It does not matter how slowly you go, so long as you do not stop.

I actually don't think this sentiment is applicable to every aspect of our lives. Sometimes it does indeed "matter how slowly you go." Sometimes you should be hustling. However, when it comes to fostering a lifetime of healthy physical fitness habits, this quote is quite prudent. Unlike other life goals (e.g., in business or personal productivity where hustling can be more beneficial), fitness goals are typically best fostered by a commitment to slow and steady progress. For most people, this is the only sort of workout regimen they'll ever need. Via this methodology, you probably won't win an Olympic gold medal. But what you will be is *fit* and *healthy* and *strong* for life.

Ch. 10: Kaizen and Your Relationships

The Weather Man

In Paramount Pictures' 2005 comedy-drama *The Weather Man*, we are introduced to Chicago weatherman David Spritz and his estranged wife Noreen. As evidenced by their contentious opening dialogue, the couple's relationship is on the rocks:

Noreen: Don't forget the tartar sauce.

David: Just call the order in, Noreen. And quit busting my you-know-what, okay?

Noreen: You always half-listen to what I'm saying to you!

David: I heard you. Tartar sauce. Tartar sauce. Tartar sauce.

Later that night, David arrives home and realizes that he has forgotten to buy tartar sauce. In an attempt to salvage the evening, he lies to his wife about his absentmindedness.

Noreen: Where is the tartar sauce?

David: They were out. They apologized. They were cool about it.

Noreen: They were out? They were out of tartar sauce? I'm calling them!

David: Noreen!

Noreen: It's not about the tartar sauce. It's about you. You don't care!

A long argument then ensues, stressing their relationship and further pushing their marriage into troubled waters.

In considering the preceding bit of dialogue, ask yourself:

- Does this discourse sound familiar to you?
- How many times have you heard couples fighting in a similar fashion—screaming at each other over an inconsequential mishap?
- Have you ever been in a comparable confrontation with your own spouse or significant other?

In this section, we'll describe four principles that will help you to avoid inciting similar relationship blunders by applying our newfound knowledge of Kaizen, Lighchi, and Hansei.

Principle #1: A big relationship problem is often the result of many little relationship problems

Arguments of the sort portrayed in comedy-dramas like *The Weatherman* are humorous because we all infer an existing underlying subtext. We know that the couple is not really arguing about a petty incident like forgetting the tartar sauce. Instead, the husband's bout of absentmindedness was merely the match in the powder barrel—the spark that ignited a store of relationship problems that had been accumulating for a long time. Or, to put it another way, the *tartar sauce incident* was merely the "final straw that broke the camel's back."

Figure 33 - Complex life problems—especially of the sort that affect interpersonal relationships—are usually incited by multiple causes. Arguments (about seemingly minor issues) may be agitated by previously existing circumstances.

This proverb is meant to describe how the sum of many small actions can eventually result in a big problem. Sometimes the causal chain of events is not obvious to all observers. In attempting to determine why the camel's back broke, consider the following potential solutions:

- The last straw weighed more than any of the previous straws.
- The last straw contained a toxic element.
- The addition of the last straw caused the camel's accumulated load to exceed the amount it could tolerate.

Obviously, the third statement best describes the reality of the situation. But, when it comes to more complex affairs, the most accurate causal explanation is often unclear to the observer—whose analysis is influenced by the perspective from which he viewed the event. Often, the narrative he devises to describe the situation may be flawed.

In *The Weather Man*, David Spritz makes this mistake when attempting to discern the cause of his collapsing marriage. In a state of exasperation, he sullenly asks himself:

What if I had remembered the tartar sauce? Would things be different?

This humorous rumination is indicative of the types of causal errors that couples so often make when attempting to assess their marital woes. Here, David has committed a *reduction fallacy*—focusing on prima facie points of contention instead of taking a moment to consider antecedent conflicts which might have contributed to the divorce.

Interpersonal relationship problems rarely originate from a single source. A lovers' quarrel may start small—perhaps triggered by an innocuous event or a tongue-in-cheek comment. But the conflict can rapidly progress into more contentious territory—like financial difficulties, child-rearing disputes, or problems with the mother-in-law. Day-to-day disagreements (about seemingly minor issues) are readily amplified by dissident undertones—echoes of past battles waged.

The trick to mitigating marital conflict escalation lies in first improving one's skill at determining its root cause. Engineers use Root Cause Analysis (RCA) to identify the multiple contributors that come together to incite a calamitous event—like a plane crash, a traffic collision, a power grid failure, or an accident with a camel.

Many techniques may be used to suss out the cause of a conflict. For starters, we can try Sakichi Toyoda's "Five Whys" method (as described in Chapter 5). To shine some light upon our weatherman's dilemma, consider the following exercise:

Why were David and Noreen fighting?

1. **Why**? - Because David forgot to buy tartar sauce.
2. **Why**? - Because he was distracted while en route to the store and his mind didn't maintain the mental note in his intermediate memory. Hence, he neglected to tell the clerk to add tartar sauce at the checkout stand.
3. **Why**? - Because he is absentminded and didn't take additional care to write down his wife's request before leaving the house.
4. **Why**? - Because he asserted his belief that he could remember to get tartar sauce via his mental note alone, and he didn't like the way his wife was nagging him about his propensity for absentmindedness.
5. **Why**? - Because the couple has communication problems and neither one believes that the other truly respects their individual contributions to the relationship.

The "Five Whys" technique is useful because it forces the mind to dig deeper — "to get to the heart of the matter." It helps us to consider multiple antecedents and determine if the petty conflict of the day is actually a proxy war—a battle resulting from ancillary issues that have yet to be properly addressed. Given the complexity of interpersonal dynamics, bringing these issues to light is often easier said than done.

Developing a personal Hansei ritual (as discussed in Chapter 2) will facilitate this task. Recall that Hansei encourages us to engage in contemplative self-reflection in an attempt to identify the source of our shortcomings. Most importantly, we strive to examine our own inadequacies *before* we attempt to assign blame to others. In doing so, the ritual helps us to overcome two deceitful cognitive biases.

- **First**, it helps us to avoid the "blame game." Even if you're convinced that you have not committed any act of malfeasance, the Hansei ritual prompts you to take a moment to consider that you *might* be at least partially to blame. By forcing the mind to occupy this theoretical headspace, you'll be more likely to see things from your spouse's perspective.
- **Second**, Hansei calls upon us to sidestep the natural tendency to fixate on the proximate cause of a disagreement. Maybe your wife wasn't angry at you because you forgot to pick up something at the store. Maybe her anger was the result of other more pressing relationship problems that have yet to be vocalized.

As discussed in Chapter 1, the big problems in life are rarely incited by a single solitary event. Instead, personal catastrophes are often the final result of a long and cumulative process—i.e., Lingchi ("death by a thousand cuts.") By developing an awareness of our faults and preventing unattended relationship problems from persisting, we can prevent little squabbles from turning into hostile conflicts—stopping the bleeding before the wound becomes fatal.

Principle #2: Relationships call upon both parties to contribute 110%

Recall that one of the original Kaizen objectives was to improve communication between individuals who worked at different levels in a corporate hierarchy. As discussed in Chapter 8, William Deming noticed that workers on a factory line were often well aware of production problems as they were developing. But they avoided mentioning them to upper management for fear of violating protocol. Consequently, Deming was so insistent that corporations "drive out fear" from the workplace that he made it one of the foundational principles of his management schema.

When there are no open channels of communication between members in an organization, then individuals begin to feel like their input is not valued. Hence, they may elect to contribute a minimal amount of effort to the union—enough to get by but not enough to thrive.

Such an apathetic mindset can be especially detrimental in interpersonal relationships—which call upon members to put in 110% of their efforts, not just their perceived "fair share." The conflict that so often arises from such deficiencies is exemplified in the conclusion of David and Noreen's argument:

Noreen: It's not about the tartar sauce. It's about you. You don't care!

David: I don't care about tartar sauce? I'm trying to make a living for this family! I've got work things to think about and pressure!

Noreen: You are so selfish!

David: I would do anything for you!

Here, David makes the mistake of assuming that his financial contribution to the relationship is all that is required of him. He doesn't think that his wife's additional demands are very important, so he often disregards her input. Noreen, in turn, is frustrated that David won't attend to the simplest of requests (like asking the store clerk to add tartar sauce). She feels sidelined and doesn't think that her husband values her contributions to the relationship. The inability of the couple to convey their desires results in both parties feeling slighted, and neither one is happy in the marriage.

Is there anything we can do to improve their channels of communication?

The 110% Rule

One trick to alleviate such tensions is to employ the "110% Rule." Before you communicate with your spouse, stop and ask yourself what the interaction would look like if you were to put in 110%. That is to say, how would the dialogue go if you were contributing *more* to the discourse than what would reasonably be expected of you.

When making her request to David, Noreen flippantly stated, "Don't forget the tartar sauce." Now, in a perfect world, this might be enough to convey her wishes to her spouse. However, if she was actually giving 110%, then she might be able to perceive the interaction from a more enlightened perspective. A more charitable chain of thought might look something like this:

- David has been working all day. His brain is tired. Intimidating people have been shouting orders and assigning difficult tasks to him for the last ten hours. Yet he tolerates this labor to provide a good life for her and the children.
- David is a good husband. He is willing to drop what he's doing and walk to the store to retrieve her order.
- The streets of New York City are chaotic, full of distracting stimuli which can cause a mind to wander. It can be easy to forget to pick up a supplemental item (like tartar sauce).
- Noreen can make the pick-up task easier by writing down her request and gently asking for David's compliance—e.g., by slipping a note to "add tartar sauce" into his hand and then sending him out the door with a kiss and a "thank you."

Alternatively, if David was also giving 110%, he might surmise a parallel set of deductions.

- Noreen takes care of the children all day. Her brain is tired. She has been transporting family members around and tending to the house for the last ten hours. Yet she tolerates this labor to provide a good home life for David and the children.
- Noreen is a good wife. She has phoned in the dinner order and is currently preparing the table for the family meal.
- The streets of New York City are chaotic, full of distracting stimuli which can cause a mind to wander. It can be easy to forget to pick up a supplemental item (like tartar sauce).
- David can ensure that he will perform the complete pick-up task by writing down his wife's instructions and verbalizing a gracious acknowledgment that he has processed her request.

If either party would have paused to step back from the discourse and conduct a more objective analysis of the situation, then the dinner argument could have been avoided. It is in this final step of the interaction that the 110% Rule should have been employed.

- David, being aware of his propensity for absent-mindedness, should carry a to-do list to remind him of his obligations.
- Noreen should appreciate that David's brain is fatigued after work. If she has an ancillary request, then she should provide him with an ancillary reminder—e.g., a written note.

By developing an intuition about your spouse's predilections, you will be better able to account for his or her less refined tendencies—thus lubricating the gears that make the household's clockwork function. Nurturing a relationship entails committing to the development of your interpersonal communication skillset, as well as a willingness to take into account the desires of your partner before those of your own.

Principle #3: Identify what triggers you

In Chapter 2, we briefly mentioned that the ancient Greeks espoused the value of reflective contemplation with the aphorism (Latinized as) *"temet nosce"* or "know thyself." It is one of the three maxims featured on the pronaos of the Temple of Apollo at Delphi—perhaps inscribed in the 4th century BC. It has been interpreted by many scholars through the ages— from Plato to Thomas Hobbes to Ralph Waldo Emerson; each posits somewhat contradictory opinions about the phrases meaning. Like so many artifacts of antiquity, we will never know the original intent of its author. But my favorite usage can be found in Alexander Pope's 1734 poem "An Essay on Man, Epistle II."

Know then thyself, presume not God to scan,

The proper study of mankind is Man.

Placed on this isthmus of a middle state,

A being darkly wise and rudely great.

In our quest for self-actualization, the most complex relationship we'll have to manage is the one with ourselves. So it is "proper" for us to take the time to perform introspection—to become intimately familiar with the drivers of our motivations, and with the light and dark angels that reside atop each shoulder.

Self-aware people know their strengths and weaknesses. They have the intuition to foresee which sets of stimuli their mind will excel at processing and which sets should be avoided.

- What irks your ire?
- What gets under your skin?

179

- What rubs you the wrong way?
- What gets on your nerves?
- What topics should you avoid discussing?

Often, the best way to prevent yourself from engaging in destructive behavior is to simply avoid putting yourself in situations that trigger it. For example:

- If you know that the morning traffic jam causes you to bark at your coworkers upon entering the office's front door, then try using the back door.
- If you know that you are too pugnacious with your spouse after a stressful work call, then avoid taking calls during family time.
- If you know that you can't have a tranquil conversation on an empty stomach, then eat something before chatting.

If you don't think such minute alterations could possibly affect your psyche, consider the following experiment. In a 2010 Columbia and Ben-Guron University paper titled "Extraneous factors in judicial decisions," researchers analyzed court rulings based on the time at which the judgment was entered. They noticed that, before the noontime lunch break, judges rarely granted parole to prisoners who were up for evaluation. However, after the lunch break, the number of paroles granted jumped up by 65 percent. In other words, these esteemed judges—men who are supposedly appointed to provide objective rulings based on evidence and reason— were actually much more lenient with their prisoners after they had a meal in their belly.

The experiment reveals how our physiological state can alter our perception of reality. "Knowing yourself" means knowing your mind as well as your body. You can get a better handle on your emotions by performing the meditative ritual discussed in Chapter 2—Hansei ("honest self-reflection"). Recall an encounter in which you disagreed with someone—like a spouse, a friend, or a colleague. Did the conversation turn into a heated argument?

- What words were exchanged that caused you to become angry?
- What could you have done to avoid or ameliorate the situation?
- Would this situation go differently in a different context?
- Would you have responded differently if you weren't so annoyed, fatigued, or hungry?
- Is it possible that the offending party was actually making some good points?

It's best to keep a journal of every interaction that succeeds in triggering you. Identify the people, places, and conversation topics that caused you to become irritable. Try to quantify the formula of stimuli and environmental conditions that incited your negative emotions.

Cataloging the perturbations of your internal world is a lifelong pursuit requiring a large repertoire of reference experiences to attune. But once this calibration is complete, you will have access to a new level of awareness and an enhanced ability to maintain a serene mindset when future foibles are encountered.

Of course, your goal in learning to identify potentially irksome situations should not be to extract yourself from *every* challenge that life presents to you. Instead, your goal should be to maintain a historical record of your "past battles lost"—so that you can modify your future strategies, compensating for your shortcomings and biases.

Often, relationship difficulties arise because couples are unable to see the world through the eyes of the other. Our mind reveals data to us via a complex tapestry; every yarn is connected to a hatchwork of memories and emotions which color the way we perceive reality. For this reason, healthy relationships are best fostered when we develop a working knowledge of the *modus operandi* of our own mind, as well as the minds of those near and dear to us. We tolerate the quirks of our family and friends because we know that the glint of a brilliant diamond can sometimes be seen in the crevices of their rough exterior. Or, as the American writer Elbert Hubbard (1856-1915) put it:

> **Your friend is the man who knows all about you, and still likes you.**

Though we will never be able to codify every grand network that coils between our ears, we can at least make an effort to enter new social situations in a state of readiness—aware of our whims, but not a slave to them.

Principle #4: Understand that relationships require acceptance of things you cannot change

Our ability to positively influence our own life outcome is limited. Even more limited is our ability to affect the life outcomes of those around us.

In *The Art of Living*, the Greek Stoic philosopher Epictetus (c. 50-135 AD) wrote:

> **Happiness and freedom begin with a clear understanding of one principle: Some things are within our control, and some things are not. It is only after you have faced up to this fundamental rule and learned to distinguish between what you can and cannot control that inner tranquility and outer effectiveness become possible.**

Similar sentiments are echoed in the famous "Serenity Prayer" written by the American theologian Reinhold Niebuhr (1892-1971). It reads:

God, grant me the serenity to accept the things I cannot change, courage to change the things I can, and wisdom to know the difference.

From time to time, we all feel inclined to try to help others. We think we can improve their situation or mend their wounds. Charity is admirable. But be advised that personal development is a quest that will not be pursued by the majority of those around you. Stagnation is the default state of man. Most people will resist aid or change—especially after they have achieved a baseline level of comfort.

Some situations cannot be improved upon. Some relationships cannot be salvaged. Instead, the correct course of action may be to let sleeping dogs lie. Acceptance is often the only gift we can give those who are estranged. Forgiveness may be all we can provide for those who have wronged us— even if they don't deserve it. This offering need not be wholly altruistic; its utility may be twofold. As Johnathan Lockwood Huie wrote:

Forgive others, not because they deserve forgiveness, but because you deserve peace.

Ch. 11: Kaizen and the Meaning of Life

Shortly after we learn how to walk, we learn how to compare ourselves to others. As the ego develops, so too does our ability to ping our environment—to gather data in an attempt to quantify our current state in the universe. Eventually, we begin to ask ourselves questions like:

- Who am I?
- Why am I here?
- Where am I going?

As we pull back the curtain of each new stage of life, these three questions persist—waiting in the wings, pining for our attention, and begging to be re-examined after every act. The scenery may change. Our role may change. Yet these three questions persist.

Our inability to provide an adequate answer to these queries can be the source of much internal angst which may manifest in the external world—affecting our attitude, our job performance, and our relationships.

- Who am I?
- Why am I here?
- Where am I going?

In formulating a response to these questions, it is typical to consider what an ideal version of yourself might look like. What could you have become if only things were a little different?

- If only you had scored higher on that exam...
- If only you had taken that job offer in London...
- If only you had married your first love...
- If only you had practiced the tuba every weekday after dinner...
- If only...

The current position in which we find ourselves is the inevitable result of the million little decisions that we made along the way. As our lifestyle choices accumulate, they formulate a trajectory that becomes increasingly difficult to alter with each passing year.

In the aforementioned film *The Weather Man*, Nickolas Cage's character ponders this predicament:

I remember once imagining what my life would be like; what I'd be like. I pictured having all these qualities—strong positive qualities, that people could pick up on from across a room. But, as time passed, few [of those qualities ever became any of the] qualities that I actually had. And all the possibilities... all the sorts of people I could be... all of them got reduced every year—to fewer and fewer. Until finally they got reduced to one—to who I am. And *that's* who I am.

Each of us keeps an image of our idealized self in the gallery of our mind. A glossy Polaroid of a smiling overachiever. If we look in the mirror and squint our eyes hard enough, we might even catch a glimpse of this person—that younger, stronger, healthier, happier, thinner, and more attractive version of ourselves. Our dashing doppelgänger. The one who succeeds in everything he sets out to do and always looks great doing it. The one who spends his life in a state of perpetual bliss—surrounded by creature comforts and lovely creatures. We might think to ourselves that if we could just become "that guy," then our life would be complete.

In waging life's many battles, we seek out this ideal version of ourselves. As we forge across the Rubicon, we carefully position each stepping stone. They form a bridge to the opposite bank—the supposed residence of our superior other.

- When we enroll in college, we envision our future self as a successful professional.
- When we get married, we envision our future self as a loving spouse.
- When we have children, we envision our future self as a wise and respected parent.

Such milestones are appropriate and healthy to pursue. But, as the American journalist Allen Saunders wrote (and John Lennon popularized):

Life is what happens to you while you're busy making other plans.

Things don't always work out as intended.

- Perhaps college proved to be too difficult or too expensive.
- The spouse that was supposed to materialize on your 23rd birthday never showed up.
- And, consequently, neither did the children.

Failures of this sort can bring about depression or anxiety. Our day-to-day tragedies make it all too easy for us to forget the many gifts that we are blessed with. Since there is no objective metric by which to gauge our current position in the game of life, our attempt to discern if we are "winning or losing" is necessarily subjective and reliant upon input that is modulated by the perceived success of those around us.

Our ancestors of the Pleistocene lived in small groups of 25 people. Calculating positions in the social hierarchy was easier for them. However, our attempt to compute the same metric is complicated by the nature of our current media-saturated world. We all carry devices in our pockets that allow us to instantly compare our own lives to the lives of everyone in town, and even to the lives of people who reside on the other side of the planet. Perhaps the ease by which such comparisons can be made is the cause of our perpetual discontentment.

The Golden Globe-winning series *Ally McBeal* featured a 27-year-old anxiety-ridden lawyer who spent each show engaged in a frenzied pursuit of the perfect career and the perfect relationship. In Season 5, Ally finally breaks down—lamenting her inability to achieve each one of her life goals:

All I ever wanted was to be rich, and to be successful, and to have three kids, and a husband who was waiting home for me at night to tickle my feet... And [now] look at me! I don't even like my hair.

Such ponderings are humorous in their acknowledgment of the absurdity of our contemporary existential dilemma. Ally's relative fortune should be clear to us all. As a young, beautiful, and well-paid Boston attorney, her life is much easier than 99% of all the humans who have walked the earth. And yet, she is repeatedly stricken down with weltschmerz—melancholy experienced when reality fails to conform to the idyllic visions of the mind.

Perhaps such sentimental ruminations are only made possible by the eradication of privation. The newfound affluence of post-World War II America facilitated the commoditization of refrigerators, dishwashers, and existential angst—as nicely portrayed in more somber 20th-century works like *Revolutionary Road* (1961) and *The Feminine Mystique* (1963). Given the steady rise in rates of suicide and drug overdose deaths among millennials, this generation doesn't seem to be coping with the new reality any better than their boomer parents did.

The French writer Michel Houellebecq—whose bouts with depression and alcoholism have become the trademark of his career—concluded his 1994 novel "Whatever" with this dreary paragraph:

For years I have been walking alongside a phantom who looks like me, and who lives in a theoretical paradise... I've long believed that it was up to me to become one with this phantom. That's done with... I am at the heart of the abyss. I feel my skin...as a frontier, and the external world as a crushing weight. The impression of separation is total; from now on I am imprisoned within myself. It will not take place, the sublime fusion; the goal of life is missed.

This stanza paints a portrait of a tortured soul. One who has spent a lifetime waiting for the "sublime fusion"—the moment of utter fulfillment when he will finally become one with the man he wants to be—the "phantom" that resides in a "theoretical paradise" of the future.

As we grow older, we may arrive at the realization that we haven't covered as much ground as we had hoped. The phantom we seek still looms ahead on the distant horizon. Perhaps we will not be able to accomplish each one of our life goals nor achieve a state of perpetual satiety.

For some, this epiphany is the source of great internal angst. Suffering the slings and arrows of life's game seems futile once one is aware of how short-lived its rewards will be.

Perhaps we shouldn't even bother trying...

Or maybe, there exists a way to reframe the game of life such that the burden of living is more manageable?

Understanding Life's Game

The pursuit of a hypothetical ideal is not a wholly unhealthy undertaking. There is a time and a place to conduct comparisons. By evaluating our status relative to that of another man (one of your competitors or even a past version of yourself), we can gauge the efficiency of our daily efforts and calculate the amount of additional work that will be required to complete our objectives. Such assessments might incite us to work harder—making us ever more vigilant in the pursuit of our goals.

Humbly comparing your efforts with those who have achieved results that are superior to your own should be a part of your weekly Hansei ritual. We ought try to better ourselves in every way. And we should take the time to imagine a better world and a better story for our lives.

But, the trouble comes when we fail to fully comprehend the nature of life's game. Like greyhounds chasing a mechanical hare around a track, the contest was never meant to be won. The hare will never be theirs.

If we constantly compare ourselves to others, then we will only succeed in casting ourselves into a state of interminable discontentment. Even if you manage to keep up with the Joneses (or leave them in the dust), know that there will always be another Mr. Jones living in the next neighborhood you upgrade to.

In the pursuit of your ideal self, you will forever be lagging. Your doppelgänger will always be a few paces ahead. The unification of your corporeal form with your projected simulacrum (the "sublime fusion" as Michel Houellebecq calls it in the preceding passage) will *never* happen. Because it was never meant to happen.

Humans are temporal beings—granted a finite amount of time in an aging body. For each mile you traverse, life will be ever-willing to introduce new and increasingly diverse obstacles into your path. Moreover, you must make this trek with a *memento mori* in your pack. Its burdensome weight reminds you that the end is nigh. Everyone who has ever lived has died. The people you love will inevitably depart from this world—quietly blinking out of existence, one by one.

Despite your best efforts to maintain order in the cosmos, the terminable nature of your brief and chaotic existence is a reality that you must learn to live with. If your happiness hinges upon your ability to achieve and maintain supremacy or stasis, then you will forever be dissatisfied. As the philosopher Sam Harris wrote:

Even when everything has gone as well as it can go, the search for happiness continues, the effort required to keep doubt and dissatisfaction and boredom at bay continues, moment to moment. If nothing else, the reality of death and the experience of losing loved ones punctures even the most gratifying and well-ordered life.

Our health, wealth, and relationships will always be vulnerable to life's many potential tragedies. Our most well-laid cornerstones can be deformed by illness, abuse, financial destitution, and unpredictable catastrophes—perhaps incited by nothing more malevolent than the whims of the weather.

The phone rings during dinnertime on some idle Wednesday. Its message shakes us to the core and topples even the most fortified foundation.

Cracks appear in the bricks of our walled garden. The ground shakes and upturns the stones that comprise the pretty path we spent so much time tending to. Some of the fault lines will run deep, and we will have no way to fully repair them. No choice but to obscure the fissure with a faux finish—enough to make it presentable, but not enough to make it whole again.

As the English novelist Paula Hawkins wrote:

The holes in your life are permanent. You have to grow around them, like tree roots around concrete; you mould yourself through the gaps.

Every fortress of man's construction will inevitably fall. If not toppled by misfortune or malice, then by the shifting sands of time. At best, you might achieve a stalemate with your idealized phantom—running alongside him, even keeping pace with him from time to time. But, in the days to come, he will inevitably pull ahead. And further down the road, in the years to come, your phantom will be nearly out of sight, so far down the path that you will have no chance of ever catching up to him again.

While this goal of achieving a state of perpetual satisfaction will forever remain elusive, the Kaizen methodology provides us with an alternate metric by which to gauge our position in the game of life. When faced with a challenge, you can choose to sit and feel sorry for yourself—dreaming of a fantasy world in which all of your life problems are effortlessly eradicated.

Or, you can get busy and take action in pursuit of your goals.

Recall the initial Kaizen question that we are to ask ourselves when considering a new objective:

What small step could I take today which may (in the long run) improve my situation?

If yesterday was a day of total inactivity, then literally *any* step taken today will be better than our past performance. Even if our subject only succeeds in engaging in productive efforts for a measly ten seconds today, that's still ten seconds more than he did yesterday.

Yesterday   **Today**   **Tomorrow**

Though his daily actions may initially seem inconsequential, we must remember that each successive day should be slightly more ambitious than the day before. Thus, over time, a ten-second workout should evolve into a ten-minute workout. And these sessions should keep compounding until our subject is executing a full-fledged fitness regimen every day.

As described in previous chapters, the great utility of this method lies in its ability to incite the creation of psychological momentum—thus enabling us to expand upon our goals gradually. Such an incrementalist approach helps to prevent us from becoming intimidated by the monumental challenge that lies before us. Instead, our attention is focused on the immediate here and now.

In this schema, comparisons are necessarily proximate. Success is achieved with each forward step. While we might maintain some notion of an idealized future version of ourselves (e.g., the one with the perfect body, the perfect relationship, or the perfect career), we understand that this goalpost is always moving. So, we don't define a "successful day" as one in which we "score a goal." Instead, a successful day is one in which we succeeded in mustering the tenacity needed to keep marching forward.

We need not concern ourselves with outpacing our colleagues or our neighbors or some possible manifestation of our future self. Instead, we seek to merely outpace the person we were when we closed our eyes last night.

- He is the only one we have to beat.
- He is the only benchmark by which we gauge our efforts.

As the adage states:

Compare yourself with who you were yesterday, not with who someone else is today.

Chasing Rainbows

Throughout this book, we have utilized imagery of people climbing stairs, trails, and mountains. Such scenery is useful in creating metaphors to describe the nature of the goal-achievement process. However, this imagery is also lacking. Hollywoodesque mountain climbing narratives tend to focus on the climactic rise to the top, and the moment of jubilation expressed by the victorious climbers on the summit. As the helicopter-mounted camera pans away from our heroes, the scene fades to black, and we're left to assume that everyone lived happily ever after.

But real mountain climbers rarely spend more than a few minutes atop a newly conquered peak. Their celebration is short-lived. Their remaining energy is expended on the long climb down. Additionally, our romantic tales often neglect to show us what happens to the climbers in the days following their descent.

- We don't see the laborious hike back to basecamp, nor the days of sleep and inactivity required to recover from the trek.
- We don't witness the melancholy of returning to a humdrum office job.
- Nor do we experience the lustful desire to find yet another mountain to conquer.

When drafting a narrative about the peaks and valleys of life, it is much more inspiring to end the story atop a peak than in a valley. But a lifelong commitment to goal attainment is comprised of *both*.

Whenever one mountaintop is summited, a new one is immediately visible in the hazy distance; and the climb continues. For this reason, the process of goal achievement is perhaps more akin to *chasing rainbows* than to *climbing mountains*.

When you were a child, did you ever attempt to locate the rainbow's end?

- Did you notice that the rainbow you sought after was always moving—the place where the bow met the ground was forever out of reach?
- Did you ever think that the bow was nearly in your grasp, only to blink your eyes and notice that it had been spirited away—now located just beyond the next slope?

It is natural to think that "life would be just great" if we could only seize the rainbow's vibrant colors and stand atop the greener pastures on which it resides. This, of course, is a fool's errand. A rainbow is not a trophy that can be won and stuffed away in a glass case. It exists not to be captured but to be admired from afar. Though we will never succeed in clutching its rays for long, we can make our lives *directionally better* in its pursuit.

This is the essence of Kaizen.

- We do not gauge the value of our lives based on the number of peaks we have won, but on the number of days we have climbed.
- We pledge that, regardless of the quagmire that we find ourselves in *today*, we will try to make *tomorrow* incrementally better.

So do not waste time fretting over life's innumerable demands. Instead, welcome new experiences, new competitors, and new projects with open arms. Embrace the rich texture of human emotions and desires that your mind provides to you. In doing so, you may develop a deep appreciation for the curious quirks of human psychology, and for the many vivid illusions of our conscious experience. Once you have managed to plant a few flags on a few mountaintops, you may come to genuinely enjoy the thrill of life's many contests.

As Mihaly Csikszentmihalyi wrote:

Of all the virtues we can learn, no trait is more useful, more essential for survival, and more likely to improve the quality of life, than the ability to transform adversity into an enjoyable challenge.

Conclusion

In this book, we have covered four important concepts from Japan and China: Lingchi, Hansei, Ikigai, and Kaizen. In review of past chapters, we'll take a moment to briefly summarize the wisdom contained in each topic.

- **With Lingchi ("death by a thousand cuts"), we learned that undesirable life outcomes do not typically originate from a single cause.** Rather, thousands of offenses accumulate over long periods, ultimately resulting in a disastrous outcome. Hence, we should strive to remain cognizant of each little moral foible that occurs during the day. E.g., the little white lies we tell to our spouse, the extra bag of cookies consumed during lunch, and our mornings of workplace tardiness. When counted individually, each one of these infractions is almost always benign. But, when considered in aggregate, they can be injurious to our life goals.

- **With Hansei ("honest self-reflection"), we learned why it's so important to take a moment to critically analyze our behaviors and identify areas of our life that could be improved upon.** In conducting an honest appraisal of our past performance, we hope to gain some perspective about our current strengths and weaknesses. This data helps us to plot a viable course down the path of self-improvement.

- **With Ikigai ("your true calling"), we discussed how the citizens of Okinawa, Japan find their "reason to get out of bed in the morning" by discovering a personal passion project.** While our passion may sometimes call upon us to suffer for our craft, it can also stir the forces of intrinsic motivation within us and impel us to achieve impressive feats. This mindset helps to keep us productive—even when times are tough or on the days when our muse is not so easily aroused.

- **With Kaizen ("continuous improvement"), we mastered the art of goal-setting via a commitment to daily incremental progress.** And we learned that even the most difficult obstacles can be atomized—broken down into manageable tasks to be completed bit by bit. By attacking the smallest objectives first, we build up a repository of psychological momentum which motivates us to advance on to increasingly more difficult challenges.

All four of these concepts are valuable in and of themselves. But I firmly believe that, when synergized into a single methodology, they become a powerful force for personal growth. As far as I know, this is the only book that has attempted to combine all four concepts into a single workable framework. This is unfortunate. Because it would be challenging to implement just one of the principles without studying the others concomitantly.

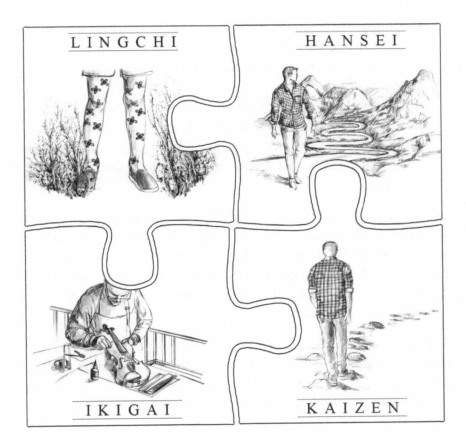

Each idea complements the other.

Each one is lacking without the other.

- **Lingchi** can teach us to recognize the pernicious effects of each tiny life transgression. But without **Hansei**, we might not know the best way to interpret this information, nor how to devise a plan to improve our situation.
- **Hansei** enables us to look back and thoroughly evaluate our personal shortcomings. But without **Kaizen** and without our **Ikigai**, we might have trouble determining how to make our future journey more profitable and spiritually fulfilling.

- **Ikigai** will teach us to find our true calling. But without the guidance of **Kaizen**, we may falter in our commitments and fail to execute the many steps that are required to become a master of our craft.

- **Kaizen** will turn us into more efficient and productive workers. But if we have a misaligned **Ikigai** (i.e., if we hate our meaningless job), then we're just another wage slave—pushing papers across a desk instead of gifting the planet with our true talents.

I hope I was able to convince you of the value to be garnered when these four concepts are working in unison. Hopefully, you are now in a better position to cite the many inefficiencies of a conventional goal-setting paradigm. Such schemas often prompt the practitioner to incorrectly frame the problem—glamorizing the process and reducing it to that of a Hollywood movie montage.

The Rocky film series perfectly exemplifies this perversion. It tells the story of a down-and-out boxer who sets a lofty goal for himself, and then completes this goal in under two hours. Sylvester Stallone wrote the original Rocky script in just three days—after watching the *Ali versus Wepner* fight at the Richfield Coliseum in 1975.

Since the film's original release, eight additional sequels have been made. The films vary wildly in production quality and watchability. But each one showcases a three-minute training sequence featuring Rocky engaged in various endurance challenges including lifting weights, eating raw eggs, chasing chickens, punching meat, sparring, and (most famously) sprinting up concrete steps. All of these exercises are performed while Rocky's theme song "Gonna Fly Now"—written by Academy Award-winning composer Bill Conti—plays in the background.

Figure 34 - Sylvester Stallone famously raced up the 72 stone steps at the Philadelphia Museum of Art in the 1976 film *Rocky*.

Such fast-paced film sequences are considered to be an essential ingredient in contemporary sports films. As evidenced by Stallone's box office receipts, it appears that many of us are mesmerized by the display of a lone man punching his way to victory against impossible odds. The 72 stone steps leading up to the entrance of the *Philadelphia Museum of Art* have been nicknamed "The Rocky Steps" because tourists come to mimic Rocky's inspirational climb to the top.

I like this film. I think just about everyone does. However, when it comes to practical goal-setting, this "Rocky methodology" can be very problematic.

When people make a pledge to accomplish a new goal, they tend to romanticize the process. They might envision themselves scaling steps or studying for their exams or lifting weights—all with the same passionate fervor that is so commonly portrayed in quick-cut cinema sequences. But, as many of us have experienced after starting a new workout regime, we usually only feel like Rocky for the first thirty seconds. After that, fatigue and discomfort creep in. Suddenly your running shoes are a bit too tight, the sun is a bit too hot, and jogging around the park turns out to be pretty boring without the accompaniment of a Hollywood orchestra.

This is why we must be wary of drawing inspiration from such narratives. Our film heroes can condition their bodies into championship fighting shape after a 3-minute song. And after 120 minutes of drama, all of their life problems are solved.

But goals in the real world are seldom achieved following a dramatic final punch. Our goals often take decades to accomplish, and our path in life is laden with obstacles of ever-increasing variety.

- Did you miss your school bus?
- Did you drop out of college?
- Were you fired from your job?
- Are you late on last month's rent?
- Has your spouse left you?
- Have you been diagnosed with an illness?
- Did you have a death in the family?

It's on days like these when we are most likely to abandon our goals entirely. It's on days like these when our dreams are prone to dissipate. We often use such setbacks as an excuse to defer our commitments. And, instead of progressing incrementally forward, we elect to just stay in bed—lamenting the difficulties of life and wondering why things can't be easier.

- Wouldn't it be nice if you could just blink all your problems away?
- Or, if you could snap your fingers and gift yourself the perfect house, the perfect spouse, and the perfect set of abs.
- What if you really did live in a paradise on Earth? A place free of life's challenges; one specifically designed to keep you in a state of utter contentment.

Is this really what you want?

The Experience Machine

In his 1974 book *Anarchy, State, and Utopia*, the American philosopher Robert Nozick, devised a thought experiment in which psychologists of the future figure out how to artificially induce pleasurable stimuli in the brain. Their machine is capable of generating experiences so vivid that the rendered scenarios are indistinguishable from reality. The storylines can even be tailored to the preferences of the subject. With the push of a button, he could be hang-gliding over the Grand Canyon, commanding a tank battalion, or racing a Porsche 918 Spyder down the Autobahn.

Figure 35 - In Robert Nozick's thought experiment, a subject is asked if he would prefer to live out his days in a virtual environment capable of simulating limitless pleasurable experiences.

And now comes the big question:

If given the option, would you choose to live out your days in the real world, or spend each moment hooked to Nozick's

"experience machine" — in which all of your hopes, dreams, and aspirations would be immediately satisfied?

Many variations of this thought experiment exist. But, when presented in its original form, most people choose to remain in their everyday humdrum life rather than plug into an artificial reality.

Science fiction fans should be quick to note the similarities between Nozick's simulated world and the one portrayed in the 1999 film *The Matrix*. The Wachowskis (being fans of neurophilosophy) were partially influenced by Nozick's thought experiment when they wrote the script. Near the end of their film, the antagonist (Agent Smith) reveals that the first version of The Matrix was a "paradise on earth." Men did not have to labor each day for sustenance. The Matrix provided everything its citizens desired. Consequently, the first Matrix was (as Agent Smith called it) "a disaster." People "rejected the program"—assumedly committing suicide en masse.

At some level, we all understand that a life lived in pursuit of the tactile experiences of reality (good or bad) ought be preferred to a life spent in a dream world. Such worlds need not necessarily originate from a virtual reality simulation. There are many means by which humans defer the burden of living; drug use, gambling, internet addiction, compulsive buying, alcoholism—each of these has the ability to dull the edges of reality. But such forms of escapism nullify the very point of our presence in the real world.

Though our problems are many and the burden of mere existence is sometimes unbearable, it is the quest to improve ourselves that makes life *meaningful*. As Jordan Peterson has said:

Life is hard. It's tainted by malevolence and betrayal. That can make you bitter. You need a meaning to offset that. Where is the meaning to be found? Not in rights, not in impulsive pleasures, but in *responsibility*. You take

> **responsibility for yourself... If you're good at it, you have some excess left over to take care of your family. If you're good at both of those, then you have some excess left over to take care of your community. Those are heavy burdens... The purpose of life is to find the largest burden that you can bear, and then bear it... The best way to pick up the burden is to *continuously improve yourself*. And that's where the meaning is to be found... The meaning is in the *continual self-transcendence*.**

The American psychologist Pamela G. Reed defined "self-transcendence" as:

> **The capacity to expand self-boundaries...toward a greater awareness of one's philosophy, values, and dreams...**

Indeed, what else could the point of goal setting be?

We set goals so that we may grow. To increase our current "capacity," we set sail in pursuit of our dreams—a voyage we embark on despite knowing that there is no final port of call. Though the travel brochures feature stylized renderings of the Land of Plenty (aka Elysium, Erewhon, Eden, or El Dorado), we know that this land does not really exist. It merely serves as the pretense for our quest. There will be no final destination. The journey is the destination.

The Scottish novelist Robert Louis Stevenson reflected on similar themes in his 1878 essay (appropriately titled) "El Dorado." He wrote:

> **When we have discovered a continent, or crossed a chain of mountains, it is only to find another ocean or another plain upon the further side... Little do ye know your own**

blessedness; for to travel hopefully is a better thing than to arrive, and the true success is to labor.

No matter how much money you make or how many life problems you succeed in delegating to others, you will always labor to carry a load (of some size) atop your back. No matter what happens today, there will always be another goal to complete tomorrow. Goal setting is an intrinsic part of the human experience. You couldn't stop goal setting even if you wanted to. And, as for your most vital objectives—the maintenance of your health, wealth, and relationships—these will require your input each and every day, until the day you die.

- There will be no time at which your to-do list will be blank.
- There will be no summit on which you will come to rest perpetually satiated in a state of interminable bliss.
- There will be no dramatic final crescendo in your life.

Instead, the road itself is the only thing that is guaranteed to accompany you on your journey. Along this road, there will be transient moments of happiness and grand victories that will conjure the emotions of fulfillment and pride. Such moments should be pursued. Such emotions should be received with gratitude and celebrated, all with the understanding that such emotions are (by design) fleeting. They are merely the pleasant byproducts of the pursuit of happiness. The pursuit itself will never end. When the victory party is over and the evening is done, your driver stands waiting by the door—ready to take you home and put you to bed, so that you can get up early for yet another day of work tomorrow.

As the American Buddhist monk Jack Kornfield wrote:

We all know that after the honeymoon comes the marriage [and] after the election comes the hard task of governance. In spiritual life it is the same: After the ecstasy comes the laundry.

Tomorrow will provide you with a new footrace to attend. Its route slivers up an endless incline—graced with only occasional points of inflection. Along this slanted path you will trek. The muscle strain from the weight of your pack superseded only by the *exhilaration of discovery*, and the promise of a new journey—whose conclusion is yet unwritten.

This is how you will awake each morning—caught in this human dilemma.

This divine quandary…

In Greek mythology, Sisyphus woke to find himself in a comparable predicament. Hades (the king of the underworld) condemned him to roll a boulder up an incline for eternity, only to have it roll back down again each time he reached the summit. When it comes to human achievement, the mind operates in much the same manner. Each time you succeed in attaining a life goal, you will be granted a temporary hiatus. But, while you are resting, the boulder of your labor will skid down to its default position, prompting you to start the daily grind all over again.

Thankfully, with Kaizen, we can learn to manage this Sisyphean struggle. And if you can discover your Ikigai (your "true calling"), then there is great pleasure to be had in your *labor of love*.

The French philosopher Albert Camus arrived at a similar epiphany following his own attempts to reconcile the plight of Sisyphus. He concluded:

I leave Sisyphus at the foot of the mountain… One always finds one's burden again. But Sisyphus…concludes that all is well… Each atom of that stone, each mineral flake of that night-filled mountain in itself forms a world. The struggle itself—toward the heights—is enough to fill a man's heart.

One must imagine Sisyphus happy.

Journey well.

Did you like the book?

Thank you for coming along for the ride with me. I really hope you enjoyed the book. If so, then please consider writing a book review. For an independent author like me, book reviews mean *everything*, and I personally read each one.

Or, if you have any suggestions on how I can improve my next book, contact me via my website at AnthonyRaymond.org. I look forward to hearing from you.

Thanks again,

Anthony

Thank you

x *Anthony Raymond*
Anthony Raymond

www.AnthonyRaymond.org

Made in United States
Troutdale, OR
12/06/2023